Alexander J. Harrison, Charles Bradlaugh

Secularism

Report of a Public Discussion between Alexander J. Harrison and Charles

Bradlaugh, held in the New Town Hall, Newcastle-upon-Tyne - Vol. 28

Alexander J. Harrison, Charles Bradlaugh

Secularism
*Report of a Public Discussion between Alexander J. Harrison and Charles Bradlaugh,
held in the New Town Hall, Newcastle-upon-Tyne - Vol. 28*

ISBN/EAN: 9783337126315

Printed in Europe, USA, Canada, Australia, Japan

Cover: Foto ©Andreas Hilbeck / pixelio.de

More available books at **www.hansebooks.com**

SECULARISM.

REPORT

OF

A PUBLIC DISCUSSION

BETWEEN THE

REV. ALEXANDER J. HARRISON,

(Minister of the Methodist New Connexion,)

AND

MR. CHARLES BRADLAUGH,

(President of the National Secular Society,)

Held in the New Town Hall, Newcastle-upon-Tyne, on the Evenings of Sept. 13 & 14, 1870.

Umpire :
LIEUT.-COL. PERKINS.

Chairmen :
For Rev. A. J. Harrison—Mr. W. TURNBULL.
For Mr. C. Bradlaugh—Mr. J. WATSON.

LONDON :
AUSTIN & CO., 17, JOHNSON'S COURT, FLEET STREET, E.C.

1870.

Propositions.

First Night:—"THAT SECULARISM, DISTINCTIVELY CONSIDERED, IS NOT A SYSTEM OF TRUTH, AND THEREFORE, CANNOT JUSTIFY ITS EXISTENCE TO THE REASON."

Second Night:—"THAT SECULARISM, DISTINCTIVELY CONSIDERED, IS NOT A SYSTEM OF MORALITY, AND THEREFORE, IS UNWORTHY OF TRUST AS A GUIDE."

DISCUSSION ON SECULARISM.

FIRST NIGHT.

PROPOSITION :—" THAT SECULARISM, DISTINCTIVELY CON-
SIDERED, IS NOT A SYSTEM OF TRUTH, AND, THEREFORE,
CANNOT JUSTIFY ITS EXISTENCE TO THE REASON."

Col. PERKINS (Umpire).—Gentlemen: The object of the
meeting this evening, and the subject to be discussed, are of
such an important character, that I earnestly hope the meeting will weigh well every word that is said, and give to
each speaker a free, fair, true, impartial, old-English hearing. (Cheers). It cannot be denied that one of the
greatest privileges that we enjoy in this country is the right
of public meeting—(cheers)—and it behoves us to cherish
and protect that right with the most affectionate and con-
siderate care ; and the way to prove that we appreciate that
inestimable public liberty, is on all occasions to show respect and impartiality to the speakers. (Cheers.) If this
is necessary upon ordinary occasions, it is more necessary
when questions like those which are about to be discussed,
this evening, are brought under consideration. (Hear, hear.)
No doubt many things may be said, many logical principles
enunciated, and many doctrines supported which may perhaps appear startling, and perhaps—even to those who
who have considered them well—rather perplexing. It is,
therefore, necessary, when listening to such a discussion as
that of this evening, we should give more attention than
usual to the subject before us, and not let our enthusiasm
carry us away from the matter in hand. The proceeds of
the discussion, after defraying certain specified expenses,
will be given equally to three public institutions of this
neighbourhood,—two in this town and one in the adjoining

borough of Gateshead; and when I mention their names I think you will feel justified in assembling under any inducement that afforded you an opportunity of assisting these institutions: the Newcastle and Gateshead Dispensaries and the Children's Hospital. (Cheers.) It is a gratifying thing to see such a crowded meeting, and I feel sure that we shall not only have a great intellectual treat, but we shall also have the satisfaction of knowing that we have assisted in supporting the institutions to which I have alluded. I therefore beg of you to listen to the speakers with as much order and quietude as possible, and also to give as little utterance to your feelings as you can. (Hear, hear, and applause.) [The Umpire then read the conditions of the discussion, as agreed upon by the joint committee.]

Mr. W. Turnbull (Chairman for the Rev. A. J. Harrison).—Mr. Umpire, Ladies, and Gentlemen: After the very proper observations to which you have just now listened, I think it would be very improper in me to supplement what has already been said with reference to this debate. I will be excused if I say—and I must say it in compliment to both disputants—that this discussion does not originate in any personal antipathy, but it is to prove the truth and nothing else. (Cheers.) I hope they will remain as friendly when they have finished the debate as when they commence it. Though chairman for Mr. Harrison, I shall be anxious to claim for Mr. Bradlaugh all that fairplay which, as an Englishman. he has the right to claim. (Hear and cheers.) Just another word, and that is, that I have faith in my man. (Cheers.) I believe he is sincere and honest, and would advocate nothing but that which commends itself to his enlightened understanding; and in the next place I think he is able to do that which he has undertaken to perform on this occasion. In your hands then I leave both the disputants, knowing that they will be listened to with fairness, attention, and kindness. (Loud applause.)

The Rev. A. J. Harrison.—Mr. Umpire, Messrs. Chairmen, Ladies, and Gentlemen: Perhaps a few words from me to-night may not be entirely useless, in regard to the reason that brings Mr. Bradlaugh and myself on this platform. It is well that this should be rightly understood by the audience, in order that no side issues may arise, either on my part or his in the discussion in which we are about to engage. It is well known that I have several times lec- tured on Secularism, and it is also well known that I have lectured upon what appeared to me to be Mr. Bradlaugh's Secularism. On several occasions I have been challenged to discuss with Mr. Bradlaugh himself, on certain subjects. These challenges, I tell you frankly here to-night, I for the most part declined ; but some time since I was challenged by the Newcastle Secular Society, in effect to state in Mr. Brad- laugh's presence what I had elsewhere stated, especially con- cerning Secularism as represented by himself; and I trust my Secular friends will not consider it a mark of cowardice when I say that this debate is not of my seeking, and that I would very much have preferred, as a matter of personal feeling, and also as a matter of personal conviction, to simply go on in my accustomed way of lecturing, and allow- ing questions to be asked at the close of each lecture (espe- cially remembering that I am not a professional lecturer, and have but little time to devote to the subject). But, when I remembered that Secularists themselves would feel that their system had hardly been fairly dealt with until I had met in public debate some responsible leader of Secular- ism, in whose ability, and experience, and knowledge of the subject, they were able to place confidence—I thought upon the whole it would be better to accept the challenge ; and not only so, but upon another ground : I considered that inasmuch as any local Secularist could come to my lecture when he pleased, it was not fair to put Mr. Bradlaugh in the same position, as he could not come except at considerable expense, and, moreover, he is professionally engaged in work of that kind, and I could not expect him to meet me simply at the conclusion of an ordinary lecture. And as I never shrink from saying to any man's face that which I say behind his back, I am glad of the opportunity of saying in substance now, what I have said elsewhere.

(Loud applause.) The proposition for discussion this evening, as already stated, is this : " That Secularism, distinctively considered, is not a system of truth, and, therefore, cannot justify its existence to the reason." This proposition naturally divides itself into two parts, and the arguments by which the proposition is proved may be divided into two parts also. First of all—that Secularism, distinctively considered, is not a system of truth. I will state the argument by which I shall, at all events, attempt to sustain the position to-night in three sentences. The first is that Secularism claims to be a system, that is, a system of truth ; the second is that if you take from Secularism all that does not belong to it, distinctively considered, there is nothing but Atheism left, and therefore, that Secularism, distinctively considered, is Atheism. The third is that inasmuch as Secularism, distinctively considered, is Atheism, it cannot be a system of truth ; first, because it has no truth to offer, and, secondly, because it is not a system at all. (Cheers.) The second part of my argument may be stated in this way, that, in the first place, for the justification of any alleged system, the so-called system must in fact be *a* system, and not only so, but *the* system which it professes to be ; in the second place, that Secularism, distinctively considered, being in reality Atheism, is neither the system it professes to be, nor in fact a system at all; and therefore, in the third place, that Secularism, as such, cannot justify its existence to the reason. Now this is the general statement, which I give for the sake of perfect clearness and fairplay, and moreover, in order to let Mr. Bradlaugh know distinctly and specially each point in my general argument, that he may see clearly and distinctly what points must be answered in order to a fair discussion ; and moreover that there may be no surprises on this question, or the introduction of matter after my first speech which properly belongs to this. Having thus stated my general argument, I will proceed to maintain it in detail. (Cheers.) In the first place, I maintain that Secularism claims to be a system of truth. I suppose I do not need to say much on the last word, for it would be a very extraordinary thing if Secularism claimed to be a system of error; but it is necessary to show that it does claim to be a system, inasmuch as this has been denied. Well now, Mr. Watts has a little pamphlet which is entitled "The Philosophy of Secularism," and I appeal to your own judgment whether that which claims to have a philosophy does not, in fact, claim to have a system; for it were a strange philosophy, indeed, if it had no system in it. Mr. Holyoake has also published a work on the "Principles of Secularism." Well now, if Secularism claims to have certain principles, I think it must be apparent that in so claiming, it claims to be a system. Further, Mr. Bradlaugh, himself, speaks of Secularism as teaching certain laws. Well, that which claims to have a philosophy, to have principles, and to teach laws, does in effect, whether the precise words be used or no, claim to be a system. (Applause.) I suppose there is no need for much further argument on this point, for is not Mr. Bradlaugh here to-night for the express purpose of maintaining that Secularism is a system, namely, a system of truth; and if Mr. Bradlaugh were not prepared to defend that, I suppose he would find, with Othello, "his occupation gone," and like the French army, he would have no choice but to capitulate as gracefully as possible. (Laughter and cheers.) So much for the first argument. My second position is, that if there be taken from Secularism, that which does not properly belong to it, there is nothing left but Atheism, and therefore that Secularism, distinctively considered, is Atheism. Now, in maintaining this proposition, I shall do what I shall not pretend to do in every particular instance: give the precise words of the quotation. But let me say in passing, that if any quotation I make be challenged by my opponent, I hope to give him proof to his heart's content, for I would rather that there should be no discussion at all, than disgrace myself, and the cause I represent, by appearing on a platform without the proof of my assertions. (Cheers.) Now, I will ask you to listen for a moment while I read to you certain quotations from a debate between Mr. Bradlaugh and Mr. Holyoake. The first quotation I shall take is from page 31 of this debate. I pray you before I read this quotation, to mark the object, namely, to show that if there be taken from Secularism that which does not belong to it, distinctively considered, nothing but Atheism is left. Now there are certain things here claimed by the National Secular Society, things that are a part of the National Society's Almanack for the current year :—

1. A system of Compulsory Secular Education, so that each child may, at starting in life, be placed in a fair condition to form more correct opinions, and be fitted for more useful conduct.

2. The disestablishment and disendowment of the State Church, and the placing all religions and forms of speculative opinion on a perfect equality before the law.

3. Specially the improvement of the condition of the Agricultural classes, whose terrible state of social degradation is at present a fatal barrier to the formation of a good state of society.

4. A change in the Land Laws, so as to break down the present system by which enormous estates are found in few hands, the many having no interest in the soil, and to secure for the agricultural labourer some share of the improvement in the land he cultivates.

5. The destruction of the present hereditary Chamber of Peers, and substitution of a senate containing life members elected for their fitness, and therewith the constitution of a National Party intended to wrest the governing power from a few Whig and Tory families.

6. The investigation of the causes of poverty in all old countries, in order to see how far unequal distribution of wealth or more radical causes may operate. The discussion in connection with this of the various schemes for social amelioration, and the ascertainment if possible of the laws governing the increase of population and produce, and affecting the rise and fall of wages.

Now there is a programme of secular work, and I ask this question of the great and enlightened audience assembled here this evening : Whether Mr. Bradlaugh, or any of the Secularists, so-called, in Great Britain, is prepared to prove here, or in any other place, that these six points in the National Secular Society's Almanack, are peculiar to those who are distinctively called Secularists? (Hear, hear, and applause.) That is the point I wish settled to-night, and upon which I hope there will be a full and fair discussion. I suppose there is not one in this audience, I care not what his creed or no-creed may be, that will not say in a single sentence that there is nothing in these six points, but such work as any social and political worker might engage in, only provided that it be consonant with the views that he holds, politically rather than religiously, and which he holds as a citizen of this country, as an Englishman, and not at all in his theological character. (Applause.) Are we, for example, to have it assumed that it is necessary to become a sceptic in order to advocate a compulsory system of education? Are we to suppose, for a moment, that it is necessary to become a sceptic in order to do that work? Is Mr. Robjohns a sceptic? Is Mr. Rutherford a sceptic? Am I a sceptic myself? for I have stood upon the platform of the League to advocate this particular thing. Can it then be said that it is necessary to become a sceptic in order to advocate a compulsory system of education? And so with the other points. There is absolutely nothing in these six points taken from this almanack to distinguish Secularists, so-called, from any other social and political workers, (Applause.) My next quotation is from page 14 of this debate between Mr. Holyoake and Mr. Bradlaugh. Mr. Bradlaugh asks :—

" How can you have your Secular entrenchments, for what is your Secularism going to do? It is going to teach men, as Mr. Holyoake explained in his very able exposition of Secularism in the Cowper Street debate with Mr. Grant, 'the Physical Laws on which health depends ; the Moral Laws on which happiness depends ; the Intellectual Laws on which knowledge depends ; the Social and Political Laws on which material prosperity and advancement depend ; the Economic Laws on which wealth depends.' "

Now, sir, these are precisely the laws that every man in this great hall ought to make it his business to study, and I contend there is absolutely nothing in this to characterise the Secularists, and to distinguish them as a body or community of persons from the great body of Englishmen in this country. It may be that we are not agreed as to what these laws are. That is quite a different thing. But are we not to study these laws, to master them to the utmost of our power, as every man in this hall will see? It seems to me perfectly absurd to think that either of these quotations I have made has the slightest characteristic mark which distinguishes Secularists, so-called, from any other persons in this country. And now I pass from that to another quotation made by Mr. Bradlaugh to the following effect:—"Although at present it may be perfectly true that all men who are Secularists are not yet Atheists, I put it to you as also perfectly true, that, in my opinion, the logical consequence of the acceptance of Secularism must be that the man gets to Atheism, if he has brains enough to comprehend." Now when we take away from Secularism those things held in common, there is absolutely nothing left but Atheism. Let us see if we can get any further authority for this. In an article entitled "What is Secularism?" Mr. Charles Watts asks whether Mr. Bradlaugh is not right in his particular views on the subject : whether the logical definition of Secularism is not Atheism. Well, sir, if Atheism be the logical definition of Secularism, then by every law of logic, Secularism cannot be either more or less than Atheism, for a definition must tell " the truth, the whole truth, and nothing but the truth;" there must be neither more nor less ; and if the logical definition of Secularism be Atheism, my proposition is distinctly proved that Secularism, distinctively considered, is Atheism. (Cheers.) Now I pass on to my next point, that inasmuch as Secularism is Atheism, it is not, and cannot be, a system of truth ; in the first place, because it has no truth to offer, and in the second place, because it is not a system at all. In the first place, " no truth to offer." Now suppose you ask a Secularist any question concerning the existence of God, or concerning the immortality of the soul, the answer given is either " I don't know," or " I deny." Well, now, ignorance and denial certainly are not knowledge; and the only thing you can possibly get out of Atheism is either confession of ignorance, or positive assertion of denial. (Applause.) But you may say, " Let us pass on to other subjects, questions concerning the constitution of the universe, or questions concerning human nature." I assert that Atheism says nothing here either, because the moment you come to consider the question of the constitution of the universe, or any question concerning human nature, that moment you pass into the region of positive science, or of mental philosophy, and I believe in positive science and mental philosophy as much as any Secularist on the face of the earth. (Applause.) So then, it appears that you cannot get any truth from Atheism; it is simply a negation and has no truth to offer. And again, I affirm it is not a system at all. Now, it appears to me, if you will consider Atheism clearly, there are only three forms in which you can put it. It may take the form of doubt, in which the mind for the time being is suspended in its judgment, and does not positively affirm anything. But the Atheism of doubt! Who could build a system up out of doubts? Well then, you may take Atheism in the form of ignorance, the Atheism—let me say with perfect respect, for I do sincerely respect the man—the Atheism of Mr. Holyoake is an Atheism of ignorance, taking the words of Cooper, who says : "I do not say there is no God, but this I say, I know not." Now, I assert you cannot build up a system out of ignorance. We will take Mr. Bradlaugh's own Atheism, and I am prepared to show that Mr. Bradlaugh's does certainly appear to be a compound of ignorance and denial. (Applause and hisses.) But we have already seen that you cannot build up a system out of ignorance or denial—(I mean nothing disrespectful towards Mr. Bradlaugh, i am merely taking certain words which he himself uses, and I am endeavouring to show what ordinary conclusions are to be deduced from them)—we have already seen that you cannot build up a system either of ignorance or denial separately ; and certainly if you cannot do so out of either separately, I wonder what sort of system will be built up out of both together. (Laughter.) Therefore, it appears Secularism is not a system of truth, because Secularism, in its logical definition, is Atheism, and being Atheism it has no truth to offer, and is not a system at all. I pass now rapidly to the second part of my argument. I will at once state it, and the first position I take under the second part of my argument is this : that for the justification of the existence of any alleged system, the reason requires that it should in fact be *a* system, and be *the* system which it professes to be. I will waste no time in comments upon that principle. It is a matter of absolute necessity in the interest of truth, it is a matter of absolute necessity in the interests of free thought, that the statement and the fact shall correspond with each other. But Secularism, as I have shown, claims to be a system. I have also shown that it is *not* a system, therefore, it is not what it *professes* to be, and it is, therefore, *false* and cannot justify its existence to the reason. But not only so, it is not only *no* system, but the very word itself is a misnomer, as you will all find by referring to your Dictionaries. By no possible license can you construe Secularism into Atheism, for unquestionably the thing intended is Atheism, and therefore the name Secularism is an utterly false representation of the thing Atheism. (Applause.) Allow me, now, in drawing my half-hour's speech to a close, to say that for my part there shall be no bitterness imported into this controversy. I have endeavoured to look into this subject with perfect honesty; I have endeavoured to take up true positions. I will treat Mr. Bradlaugh himself and his arguments with perfect courtesy and respect, which are but another name for justice—for courtesy is justice. No questions of sincerity shall arise, as between him and me to night. It is not my business to question any man's sincerity, therefore I simply content myself with saying that Mr. Bradlaugh's views, whatever they may be, cannot destroy his rights as a man ; but while I admit this with perfect frankness, I have no mercy for Secularism, not a bit. I purpose to treat it with justice, but mercy it cannot deserve, for I believe— for the reasons assigned—Secularism to be mischievous and false in name, for if the thing be Atheism, let the name correspond with the fact. (Applause.) Mr. J. P. Adams, himself a sceptic, in an article written in the columns of the "*National Reformer,*" admits that Secularism scarcely appears to be an honest name. Then, in the name of honesty get rid of it. (Cheers.) Then if we come to discuss Atheism, we shall discover that Atheism is only a negation, that it has no truth to offer, and that it is not a system at all. And so, when we come to the discussion of this subject and look upon Secularism, in so far as it has

positive teaching, we shall find that it is only in common
with others, and, in so far as it is distinctive, it is merely
Atheism, and Atheism is not a system and cannot give you
any positive teaching whatever. Here then is the ground
I take to-night. I will re-state the positions I have attempted thus briefly to prove, the positions for which I
am willing to do battle to-night ; positions I hope Mr.
Bradlaugh will answer. My positions are shortly these :
First, that Secularism claims to be a system of truth ;
secondly, that if you take from Secularism that which does
not properly belong to it, there is nothing but Atheism left ;
and thirdly, Secularism therefore, being confessedly Atheism,
cannot be a system of truth, first, because it has no truth to
offer, and secondly, because it is not a system at all. And
then, under the second part of my argument, I have said
that for the justification of the existence of any alleged
system, the reason requires that it shall be in fact a system,
and not only *a* system, but *the* particular system which it
professes to be. Then I have shown that Secularism,
distinctively considered, is not the system it professes to be,
and is not a system at all, and, therefore, Secularism fails
to justify its existence to the reason. Now in all this there
is no appeal to the passions ; in all this there is the simple
question of whether my arguments be logical or not; in
all this it is a matter of right that they be decided by the
sheer application of the intellect. Whatever may arise in
this discussion, I will hold in full confidence to these propositions, and I will endeavour to maintain them. And
upon this ground I have argued that Secularism, distinctively considered, is not a system of truth, and therefore, cannot justify its existence to the reason; and this
ground I will maintain by debate, and for no consideration
will I depart from the proposition I have stated, and to
that proposition shall I confine all my energy, and all my
intellectual force this night. (Loud applause.)

Mr. J. WATSON (Chairman for Mr. Bradlaugh).—Mr.
Umpire, Brother Chairman, Ladies, and Gentlemen : I am
sure to you, as to myself, it must be a considerable gratifi-

cation to learn that in connection with this discussion, it
is not a discussion of mere personal matters, but that it is
a discussion for truth, and for that which each disputant
considers to be his own truth. I am very pleased with the
marked hearing you have given to Mr. Harrison. I say·it
argues well for the people of Newcastle-on-Tyne. I think
you might go into many meetings of this description, and
not see the audience conduct themselves as you have con-
ducted yourselves this evening. I hope, I ask, I claim for
Mr. Bradlaugh the same impartial, manly, old-English hearing that you have given to the other gentleman. (Loud
cheers.)

Mr. C. BRADLAUGH.—Mr. Umpire, Messrs. Chairmen,
and Friends: It would be the merest affectation on my
part to pretend that I was not glad of the opportunity afforded me this evening of expressing my views to you on the
subject under debate. I don't pretend to say whether this
debate is, or is not, of my seeking. I always seek debate.
(Hear, hear.) I never shun it ; I desire as much as possible
that every topic I attack shall be fairly debated. I can hardly
say now that I am not a professional lecturer, but I am only
one of three month's standing, so you must not put that too
strongly upon me. All my other work in lecturing, all my
other work in speaking, all my other work in writing has
been done in the time I could spare from earning my liveli-
hood, otherwise it is only three months ago that I determined to devote myself professionally for the rest of my life
to the task of knocking to pieces what I conceived to be error
and delusion. I am not either a leader, or the leader of the
free-thought party in Great Britain, but I believe I may
fairly say that I am one in whom they place confidence, and
therefore have some right to speak for them to-night. The
only reason why I repudiate the word "leader" at all is, that
you will find it will be utterly inconsistent with the exposition of Secularism which it will be my duty to submit to you
in this speech. Now, I have nothing to complain of in the
speech to which we have just listened, except so far as my
own views are concerned, at present, my very able antago-

nist knows nothing about them. (Hear, and cheers.) That is the only defect I see in his speech. It is to that, amongst other matters, I shall have, of necessity, to direct a portion of my reply. I don't know whether I need trouble to discuss with you what is a system, and whether Secularism be a system or not, because I think I have made it clear enough all my life through, that the great merit of the thought of which I am permitted to be the advocate is that it don't pretend that any one man, or any dozen men, have the right to lay down a number of propositions, and say "these make a system which shall bind the world." (Hear, hear, and cheers.) But on the contrary, we admit and affirm that there is no man so false but who teaches some truth, and there is no man so true but who utters some falsehood; that the best collection of truth you can make is to collect it as you would a bouquet of flowers in your garden, here one flower from one shrub, here one from another plant, here another from another bush, until at last, you have collected that which in shades of colour, and in fragrance of perfume, makes the real bouquet you want. I take heroism, if I find it in a bishop; a logical sequence even if I find it in my friend. I take in fact truth from any man, truth from whoever I can get it. I repudiate for heretics, I repudiate for Secularists, any sort of claim to a monopoly of infallibility or system-building. (Cheers.) Then there is another point that I do not know I need trouble to discuss, whether Secularism is Atheism or not, because I think it is. (Laughter and cheers.) I have always said so, I believe for the last 13 years of my life, whenever I have had an opportunity of doing so; and it is hardly likely, therefore, that I should come here to night— without any reason for so doing—to recant all my previous convictions, and to make an allegation utterly inconsistent with all my previous arguments. Then it resolves itself into this : are the declarations which I have made as to Secularism—because our friend is good enough to say that it is the Secularism of Mr. Bradlaugh which he wishes to discuss—are the declarations I have made as to Secularism inconsistent with the position I take ? And I was somewhat struck, not with any want of fairness—for our friend was fair enough—but with the peculiarity connected with his reading, what I suppose you would have understood to have been secular principles. If he has looked at the Almanack secular principles, in the 15th page he would have found the secular work; and I think I will show you that religion impedes the obtainment of any one of the objects sought to be obtained in that work. I will read to you first the matter my friend omitted—I don't mean in any unfair sense, because I suppose he will use that which will make out his case the best, and I shall probably do the same with mine. (Cheers.) The principles of the National Secular Society, as given in page 15 of the Almanack, and also stated in the debate, are these :—

1. This Association declares that the promotion of human improvement and happiness is the highest duty.

2. That the theological teachings of the world have been, and are, most powerfully obstructive of human improvement and happiness ; human activity being guided and increased by a consciousness of the facts of existence, while it is misguided and impeded in the most mischievous manner when the intellect is warped or prostrated by childish and absurd superstitions.

3. That in order to promote effectually the improvement and happiness of mankind, every individual of the human family ought to be well placed and well instructed, and all who are of a suitable age ought to be usefully employed for their own and the general good.

4. That human employment and happiness cannot be effectually promoted without civil and religious liberty ; and that, therefore, it is the duty of every individual—a duty to be practically recognised by every member of this Association—to actively attack all barriers to equal freedom of thought and utterance for all, upon political and theological subjects.

Now what does our friend do? He reads to you the programme which the National Secular Society sketched out for Secular work, and says the work is not distinctively secularistic, and therefore Secularism is not a system. Well, now, that would not prove his case even if it were true. It has in addition the defect of not being true. But if it were true, it would not do, because in addition to attacking the work we lay down, he ought to have attacked the principles which we state are to guide Secularists in doing that work. (Applause.) What is the first work we take? "A system of compulsory secular education, so that each child may, at starting in life, be placed in a fair condition to form more correct opinions, and be fitted for more useful conduct." But our friend says "that is not distinctively Secularistic, and a great many other people are in favour of Secular education." Yes, but I answer that you are in favour of it, not because of your Christianity, but in spite of it. You are in favour of it not from any principle that you can read to me from your Christian teaching, but in spite of your Christian teaching, and because of the heretical and atheistical endeavours that have been made to free the education of the world from the grip and superstition of the Church. (Applause.) Is it true, aye or no, that "the theological teachings of the world have been, and are, most powerfully obstructive of human happiness?" I say yes ; yes, they have been. I say that history corroborates me that whenever you find a nation much subject to theological teaching, that there you find it much deficient in everything that will promote general human happiness ; and I say that the nations which have the most liberty, the most thought, the most humanity are those which are freed from the effects of theological teaching. And I say, if that were not so, we ought not in the 19th century to be debating Secular education at all ; for if it were true that Secular education did not belong to the platform of heresy, which I am advocating, how is it that the Church, years and years ago, when it had every child in its own power, did not educate them? How is it that they kept them ignorant? How is it that it hindered the work of that secular education which our friend says he is anxious to do? I admit there are many good Christians working for it, just as they are working for a revision of the Bible, because they have been driven out of their old defence, they were ashamed of their old practises, and they conform to ours to-day. (Applause.) Then we will take the next : "The disestablishment and disendowment of the State Church, and the

placing all religions and forms of speculative opinion on a perfect equality before the law." Our friend says this is not distinctively secularistic. If it is not, it is a misfortune that the men who have gone " distinctively" to prison for it, in the endeavour to achieve it, have been reputed to be the most infidel in the country. I agree that to-day there is much cry for religious equality from our friend and many who work with him, and that there are some brave, true, good, honest men in every church and chapel, who, despite their Christianity, would give me as much right as I would desire to take, in the utterance of my opinions. (Cheers.) It would be folly and insanity to deny that; but I contend it is because of their humanity and not because of their religion; and if our friend dares to deny that, I will quote text after text from his own Book to show him that it is contrary to his theology. And I will ask how it is that, at the present moment if the putting of opinions on an equality before the law be not distinctively a feature of our work, and of our agitation, how it is that his Church with its power, has left that Act 9 and 10 of William III., chap. 32, to condemn me to prison for denying, as I do deny, that which my friend advocates to be true? Why, I am at the mercy of any one among you, who could convict me, and who, at the same time, happened to be sufficiently imbued with the persecuting spirit of the Old and New Testament, and who desired to do so. (Hisses and applause.) At any rate, to take our friend's own view of Secular work, that should be considered distinctively secular. Then we come to the next point :—
" Specially the improvement of the condition of the agricultural classes, whose terrible state of social degradation is at present a fatal barrier to the formation of a good state of society." Has any of our friends tried to improve them? Why, is it not a fact that while they have gone to civilize the Fijiis—inhabitants of islands hardly marked out on the maps of the world, in seas yet only partially explored—they have left the agricultural classes of Norfolk, Essex, and Sussex, of Hertfordshire, Wiltshire, Dorsetshire, Devonshire, and of Lancashire, and Gloucestershire in such a state that the parliamentary report itself asserts that they are a disgrace to

any Christian community, and more than that, in Norfolk their condition is very little above the level of the swine. I am quoting from the Parliamentary report, and I ask you whether, if that amelioration of the condition of the agricultural classes has been Christian work, why it has not been done long ago? They have all the wealth, all the power, all the talent, all the logic, all the eloquence, and we find they have not done it. Could you blame us for fancying that this was our work for the doing, when we took to it? (Applause.) The next point is as to the change in the land laws, which is to alter the present system, by which enormous estates are found in the hands of the few, while many have no interest in the soil, and to give to the agricultural labourer some share in the land he cultivates. Now I presume that our friend admitted the truth of the allegations contained in the propositions, which are that the land is in the hands of the few, and that the labourer who cultivates it the most, gets too little out of it. That I presume he admits. Then let us see whether or not it is secularistic work, and I contend that, by the Bible, our friends are prevented from giving a remedy; and if he desires it, I will quote him texts to prove it. As a matter of fact we have found the theology which my friend advocates the means of aggregating the land in the hands of the few by depriving a large majority of the people of their rights, and until we make them heretics in theology as well as heretics in politics, we believe we have no means of effectuating that grand revolution which we mean to effectuate in the next ten years, which shall crumple up the large landed holdings of this country and put them into the hands of the agricultural classes. (Loud applause.) Now I am glad that, by your last applause, you have repudiated that this is Christian work, by your expression of opinion you have declared that you don't approve of the present state of things. Now, it is hardly worth while, I presume, imagining that there are any of you who do not think that the large landed estates should not be broken up? Why, when you find the agricultural labourers with seven, eight, and nine shillings a week and the Marquis of Westminster with £1,000,000 a year, and

the Duke of Devonshire with 96,000 acres in the neighbour-
ing county of Derby, and the people driven to find their
bread across the Atlantic and the Pacific, while there are at
least 11,000,000 acres of waste land in the United Kingdom
capable of cultivation,—I say, if that be Christian work
you have been a long time in doing it, and you can hardly
wonder if we have taken it up.   Well, then, the next is :—
"The destruction of the present hereditary Chamber of
Peers, and substitution of a Senate, containing life members,
elected for their fitness."   Well, now, if our friend presumes
that that is Christian work, where will he find the slightest
indication of anything of the kind ?   Why, I will undertake
to find for him from his own book, that he is not to interfere
in any way with the governing bodies of the nation, not even
if they are wrong, and I ask him then, how can he put that
as Christian work as against Secular work ?   The last point,
however, is an investigation of the causes of poverty, with
a view to their removal.   Our friend will hardly say that that
is Christian work, when the Bible itself declares that "the
poor shall never cease out of the land;" and whether we
are right or wrong in what we are trying to do, at any rate
we are trying to do something which the Bible says never
shall be done.   But then our friend read a statement from
Mr. Holyoake's "Exposition of Secularism,"—as quoted by
myself in the debate,—which professes to teach men the
physical laws on which health depends.   Our friend cannot
say that Christianity does that, because, here is the instance
of a new sect called the "Peculiar People," who actually
have been committed to gaol for manslaughter because of
their Christianity, and of their not being Secularists, and
who did not believe in the social and physical laws upon
which health depend, for they thought that if you pray over a
man, woman, or child, it will cure them, as the Bible teaches.
(Laughter.)   My friend laughs at this, and so do I ; and I
am happy to have that illustration of the change in his
views, despite his Christianity.   Well, then, I urge that the
Bible teaches that health depends, that happiness depends,
not upon the causes upon which they are really found to
depend; but upon arbitrary questions of man's faith; and

if it were Secularistic, if it were Atheistic in showing men the real way in which health may be sought, and if my friend says that a surgeon will lead you to health I say yes, but it is in consequence of his scientific knowledge, and not in consequence of his Christianity; for his scientific knowledge is opposed by Christianity, is crushed by Christianity—

Mr. TURNBULL (rising).—Are me met to discuss Christianity or not? (Loud and protracted cheering.)

Mr. BRADLAUGH.—How am I to explain to you what is Secularistic work? (Uproar.)

The Rev. A. J. HARRISON then rose.

Mr. BRADLAUGH (to Mr. Harrison).—Sit down, sir; sit down. (More disapprobation.)

The Rev. A. J. HARRISON.—I hope—(The remainder of the sentence was interrupted by the continued noise.)

Mr. BRADLAUGH (to Mr. Harrison).—I was perfectly quiet during the whole of your speech—(interruption)—and I will say my say in my own way. (Renewed disapprobation.)

Col. PERKINS.—I am quite sure that Mr. Bradlaugh will continue his speech; he has only two or three minutes more—(Mr. Bradlaugh: Five minutes, please.)—I am perfectly willing to admit that, because of the interruption; but I am sure it his quite his limit. I hope he will conduct the remainder of this discussion in a manner which will not trench upon the feelings of my friend on the left in the slightest degree. (Applause.)

Mr. BRADLAUGH.—I will conduct this debate as I have all others during my life : in the way in which I think will best express my views. Why did our friend read these things through, one by one, if I was not to go through them afterwards, and show that they were not Christian work? (Cheers.) I am glad that his chairman has interposed, for it shows that I have struck at a weak point at once, and he deems it right to come to the rescue of his friend; but I would like our friend's chairman to remember that he and his colleague are more ornamental than useful, and that they should leave matters of that kind in the hands of the Umpire. One remark more, and I have finished. In the latter part of my friend's speech he said that my Atheism was a compound of ignorance and denial, that it was only a negation, and has no truth to offer. Well now, I think that the gentleman who made that assertion had never taken the trouble to read my " Plea for Atheism" at all, and still less taken the trouble to read what I said about Atheism in the debate with Mr. Holyoake. And, so far from my theory being a compound of ignorance and denial, it goes on, quite as distinctly as any Christian can on his side, to make affirmations which are positively inconsistent with, and which, if demonstrated, are entirely opposed to, the continuance of our friend's views at all; and it is monstrously unfair, as well as untrue, to give any such view of Atheism. It would be impossible at this late stage of my speech, to give you, at any length, a proof that my Atheism is not ignorance and denial alone. I will tell you how I put it in my " Plea for Atheism." I say that " some declare that the belief in God is necessary as a check to crime. They allege that the Atheist may commit murder, lie, or steal, without fear of any consequences. To try the actual value of this argument it is not unfair to ask—Do Theists ever steal? If yes, then in each such theft, the belief in God and His power to punish has been inefficient as a prevention of the crime. Do Theists ever lie and murder? If yes, the same remark has further force—hell-fire failing against the lesser as against the greater crime. The fact is that those who use such an argument overlook a great truth—i.e., that all men seek happiness, though in very diverse fashions. Ignorant and miseducated men often mistake the true path to happiness, and commit crime in the endeavour to obtain it. Atheists hold that by teaching mankind the real road to human happiness, it is possible to keep them from the by-ways of criminality and error. Atheists would teach men to be moral now, not because God offers as an inducement a reward by and by, but because in the virtuous act it self immediate good is ensured to the doer and the circle surrounding him. Atheism would preserve men from lying, stealing, murdering now, not from fear of an eternal agony after death, but because these crimes make this life itself a course of misery. While Theism, asserting God as the Creator and Governor of the Universe, hinders and checks man's efforts by declaring God's will to be the sole diresting and controlling power, Atheism, by declaring all events to be in accordance with natural laws—that is, happening in certain ascertainable sequences—stimulates man to discover the best conditions of life, and offers him the most powerful inducement to morality. While the Theist provides future happiness for a scoundrel on his death-bed, Atheism affirms present and certain happiness for the man who does his best to live here so well as to have little cause for repenting hereafter." I have now occupied the time which the Umpire tells me is my right, and I leave the case, making no professions of sincerity or insincerity, leaving it with you to stand or fall, and only promise that in this debate I shall follow, step by step, the line which my opponent takes. (Loud Applause.)

Mr. TURNBULL.—I have great pleasure in calling upon Mr. Harrison to address the meeting.

Rev. A. J. HARRISON.—Allow me to explain why I rose just now. As far as I am concerned there shall be no personal element introduced into this debate, and I wish to explain that I certainly did not rise for the purpose of interrupting Mr. Bradlaugh, though he might seem to think so, and I hope he will withdraw the expression he used to me :— " Sit down." I think he had no right to say that; I think it was an excitable exclamation, on account of his not understanding altogether, our position. When I rose to appeal to the Umpire—which I had a perfect right to do—Mr. Bradlaugh orders me to sit down. Well now, that is a little extraordinary, but at all events, I hope we shall not have a repetition of it. Mr. Bradlaugh began by saying that he never shuns debate. Well, as far as the duties of my position allow me, I never shun debate, though it might be a question of wisdom as to which is the best method of conducting a debate; and the fact that I have never lectured upon Secularism yet, without allowing discussion at the close of it, is sufficient proof that I do not shun debate. Moreover, in reference to myself, all I have to say is that my presence here to-night is sufficient proof that I do not shun debate with Mr. Bradlaugh. (Cheers.) He states that the works he has written and so on, were done in the time of leisure from the several pursuits in earning his bread. My lectures on Secularism were given in my times of leisure from the pursuits by which I earn my bread. He says he is not *the* leader, nor *a* leader of the Secular party. Well, I don't exactly understand that assertion. I attribute it to Mr. Bradlaugh's modesty in the matter. I mean no sarcasm, but it does appear true that he at all events, is considered by the Secularists to be *a* leader, if not *the* leader, when they have made him President of the Secular Society. (Cheers and laughter.) Furthermore, he told me that the only fault he had with my speech was that I seemed to know nothing about his views. Well now, I rather imagine it will emerge before this discussion is closed that I know too much for Mr. Bradlaugh. (Applause.) He tells me that the great merit of the free-thinking mind is that it does not pretend to accept the system of any one man, or of any dozen of men, and so on. Well, what does that mean ? It means, that either the Secularists have a system or they have not. If they have no system, what in the world are they here for to discuss to-night ? (Cheers) And, here is the very thing I should exceedingly like to know, that, if they have no system which is to bind the world, whether Secularists do not desire that the principles which they hold should be universally received, and whether they do not desire that those principles should spread all over the world;

and if so, will not there be a system for the whole world?
(Applause.) He tells us, moreover, that we are to collect
from every tree, and flower, and shrub, and—mark the
word—make them into a bouquet. Now, that is very much
like every man making a system for himself. I presume
that is the case. But if that be so, that every Secularist,
so-called, makes a system for himself, then I want to know
what need there is for a National Secular Society? (Laughter and applause.) And then again, I want to know how
you can possibly have any Secular organization, unless you
have some definite principles, which are in effect a creed or
system, whether you call them so or not. We are told that
the merit of freethinkers is, that you have expansion and
growth. But it by no means follows that a system is incapable of expansion, and that because you have a definite
set of principles, you may not go on applying those principles to the widest range. It is the very proof of a true
system that you may extend its principles to the widest
application. At least one thing has emerged very clearly
from the debate, and that is the unquestionable statement
that Secularism is Atheism. (Cheers.) Now I pray you to
understand this matter rightly and clearly; let there be no
mistake about it. In order to do Secular work properly—
and I pray you mark the words and carry them home with
you—you must, according to Mr. Bradlaugh, become
Atheists. Very well, that is the position; and I am glad
that it has come out. Now let us proceed to the application of this. Mr. Bradlaugh went on to read certain Secular principles, and I would like to know if Mr. Bradlaugh
can prove to me that those principles and that work,
through which he has gone step by step, are Atheistic?
If Mr. Bradlaugh at once admits that Secularism is Atheism,
it is not admissible to go back and use the indefinite word
Secularism whenever it suits him. Once admitted that Secularism is Atheism, we must bear this definition in mind.
Now take Mr. Bradlaugh's logic upon another point,
theology—for remember the reference to Christianity was
not introduced by me; I am not going to discuss that subject at all, not a word of it. (Cheers.) Let Mr. Bradlaugh

say what he likes, the position is this. Mr. Bradlaugh appears to contend that because some ideas which have been entertained concerning the Divine existence had been opposed to progress, that, therefore, every possible idea of the Divine existence is opposed to progress. That is very nice logic! What Mr. Bradlaugh ought to prove is, that every possible conception of God is opposed to progress, and not that this or that system or creed is opposed to progress, and that it is impossible to have a belief in God and yet have this progress. He gives us to understand that while there are many amongst us that do good work, notwithstanding our theology, that this work is not on account of our theology, but despite it. Now, what does that prove? I will answer. him in another way. I affirm that though many Atheists have done good work, it has not been on account of their Atheism, but despite it. The question we really have to discuss to-night is not whether it is possible for an Atheist to do good work or no. What I say is this : that whatever work is done in that respect is not done as an Atheist, but done as a man. Whatever may be the peculiar functions of theology in certain defined respects, it has to be shown, and in effect has to be maintained, that Theism in every possible form is absolutely opposed to progress. But supposing that he has proved that, which it is impossible for him to do, what remains? Does it follow that all this work is done by Atheists, as such? So, when Mr. Bradlaugh talks about secular education being secular work —for he says we have been driven into it—does he mean that it is atheistic work? We are to have it understood that wherever Mr Bradlaugh and his *confreres* have sought to advance secular education, it has been for the sake of making people Atheists. If Mr. Bradlaugh does not use the proper word, let him give us a clear and definite meaning. Then he tells us that we have been driven to this secular work—that we have been driven to it as a matter of compulsion. And pray, who has exercised this compulsion? It has been exercised by the magnificent forces of so-called Secularism. Why, if we have been driven to this by that party—supposing it were true—it is the greatest compliment, in one point of view, he could pay us, because in saying so, he asserts that we have been open to reason. He admits in fact that we have minds free enough, and hearts big enough to take in the thought. Moreover, he tells us that religion is the product of man in some shape, and I want to know how long the human reason has been in the world—that human reason, of which Secularism is said to be the latest and most glorious offspring—how long has it been in existence? Then he asks, why does not theology accomplish this work and that work? That is not the question. I ask: Why has man, as man, not done the work that belongs to him, as man? (Applause.) And now I ask you, taking up the points most vital and essential, whether Mr. Bradlaugh has done what he said he would do, and what he promised to do? I hope next time he will do it. But I would like to know how he can affirm that Atheism, in the true meaning of the word, has anything positive about it at all? He knows perfectly well the meaning of the word. It is simply a speculative question, based partly on ignorance and partly on doubt. Ignorance can give you nothing; doubt—take it as doubt—is not truth, but conjecture, Mr. Bradlaugh has not dealt with any part of my argument. I appeal to him to-night—believing as I do, that he wishes a thorough discussion—to take up this particular point. and to show wherein it is possible for the thing called Atheism to be positive teaching at all. For I assert that if there be anything positive about it, it does not belong to Atheists as Atheists, but to men as men. It has been assumed, again and again, that Secularists have done this and that great work, and now mark you how he chops and changes about,—now it is infidelity, now it is free-thinking, now it is atheism, and the like. But he has never told you, what it is utterly impossible to prove, that the great leaders of thought of the past were Atheists. You may call them Sceptics, you may call them Secularists, if you will, but you must define what you mean. I affirm that, in the sense in which Mr. Bradlaugh has used the term, these men were not Atheists, and not being Atheists in his sense of the word, they were not Secularists. How then, does he prove the advantages of Secularism by referring to the work which those who were not Secularists had done ? (Loud applause.)

Mr. BRADLAUGH.—I suppose it will be hardly worth while to waste time to discuss whether or not I was out of order, because if my friend and his Chairman had not rose I would not. Our friend says this debate has brought out some little reference to Secularism distinctively. Listen to what I said when I debated with Mr. Holyoake. I said :—"I hold that Atheism is the logical result to all who are able to think the matter out; but I don't hold that every person with whom I come in contact is able to come to it. Some get rid of one or two shackles of superstition, some get rid of many, but very few get rid of all. So soon and so long as a man and woman are prepared to work for human improvement, and recognise the fact that the theological systems of the present day are barriers to its attainment—which are to be broken through—so soon and so long are they fit to be co-workers in our association. We have no National Church, no hard and fast line, no creed, for those who enrol themselves as co-workers. The only work we teach is the work essential to human redemption." And I put it there as distinctly as it was possible to put it, but our friend said: "If you have no system, why have you a National Secular Society?" Why because we teach and put to the world that the theological teachings of the world have been, and are, powerfully obstructive to human happiness and improvement, and that we have got to get rid of these theological teachings. That is why we have got this society, that is why my propaganda is necessary, why my friend is here to-night; because those who listen to me and those who work with me, are increasing, and he and his party find it is necessary they should do something to stop that increase ("No"). You say no; the Bishop of London says yes, the Bishop of Manchester says yes, and the Archdeacon, delivering his Visitation Charge in this very borough, says yes. I don't know whether it is true. If you say no, I say yes, and I shall take the liberty of saying

yes, until I see the halls empty which when I left, I saw full.
Then he says he has not introduced Christianity. Pardon
me, but that the theological teachings are hindrances to human improvement and happiness ("No," and "Question.")
Well, I thought that we were met to discuss Secularism,
and I am delighted that you cannot leave it to your friend,
because it shows that I have disturbed you as well as him.
(Laughter and applause.) I think the principles of Secularism, as laid down here to-night, may be taken as our exposition as to what we mean by it. If you mean something
else, if you are only kind enough to tell me what it is, I
shall only be to happy on some future occasion to debate it.
(Laughter, hisses, and interruption.)

Mr. TURNBULL (rising and addressing the meeting.)—I
hope you will not interrupt Mr. Bradlaugh. (Renewed dis-
satisfaction, and a voice,—"It is his right.")

Mr. BRADLAUGH.—It is a right which I will take, a right
which I have fought for long enough, and a right which I
am sorry to find that, even in an audience like this, there
is need to enforce. What sort of display of such feeling
have I shown towards your advocate? At least Secular
teaching has had the effect of making men who came to
Secular lectures listen patiently while their views are attacked. (Applause.) Now this is the astounding proposition
which our friend—who is good enough to compliment me
(I suppose meaning it) on the possession of a clear and logical mind—this is the astounding proposition which our
friend submits for your consideration. He says "Mr. Bradlaugh teaches that because some conceptions of God have
been opposed to progress, that, therefore, every possible conception of God is opposed to progress." Now, Mr. Bradlaugh
don't. He teaches that all the *taught* conceptions of God
have been opposed to progress. He cannot tell what might
be possible to your conception; when you tell him what you
conceive, then he will tell you whether it is opposed to progress or not. And I assert that every preached conception
of God has been opposed to the human family. I don't

mind which of them you give me. As to chopping and changing names; they are all honourable names, and men have gone to gaol bearing every one of them, men have been burnt for holding some of them, and then you ask me whether Secularism has modified the conduct of your Church, and in triumph you say—" If it has, it at least shows that we have not been bigoted, we have been amenable to reason." Yes, but after you burnt our best men as you did Bruno at Rome. I say that all theological teaching has been opposed to, and has crushed out human thought, and instead of your being amenable to reason, the party you advocate has only been amenable to fear, and that when you could not burn them and rack them, you took and imprisoned them. And if you ask why this propaganda is necessary, it is because only a few months ago an infidel had no civil rights in the witness box at all, and even at present is liable to serious legal disqualifications if he dared be honest and true. (Cheers.) If we had religious equality, we should not now be clamouring for it; it is because we have it not that we have to urge it. Well, but you say, Atheism can be nothing but a negation; and if saying it proves it, you have demonstrated your proposition. But you have not taken the trouble to deal with the assertion I made in my former speech from my " Plea," and I will now repeat it :— " Theism declares that God dispenses health and inflicts disease, and sickness and illness are regarded by the Theist as visitations from an angered Deity, to be borne with meekness and content. Atheism declares that physiological knowledge may preserve us from disease by preventing our infringing the laws of health, and that sickness results not as the ordinances of offended Deity, but from ill-ventilated dwellings and workshops, bad and insufficient food, excessive toil, mental suffering, exposure to inclement weather, and the like—all these finding root in poverty, the chief source of crime and disease ; that prayers and piety afford no protection against fever, and that if the human being be kept without food he will starve as quickly whether he be Theist or Atheist, theology being no substitute for bread." (Cheers.) I am at a loss I confess to discover the ground of complaint arising, either in the mind of my opponent or in the minds of my auditors, from the course I took. I went through the very matter he had chosen to read, nor did he venture to grapple with any one of those propositions, or to show in what way the theological teachings of the world would affect them. And why? Because I threatened him with his own texts if he dare. My friend says I ought not to have introduced Christianity, but what is his own declaration? His own declaration is that my doctrine is Atheism, and that my doctrine is a war on his theology. Then, I ask him how can he expect to conduct a war without having his own side attacked in the battle? Does he expect that I am simply to dodge his shot, and not to send any back in return? That is not the way I have been accustomed to fight. Now, really in the last speech I asked, what have we had but your fine words? We have had a lot of talk about the magnificent forces of the so-called Securalists, and I ask him how it is that, in every age of the world the leaders of thought have been persecuted by the leading theologians of the age? Why it is that, in their lifetime they have been denounced as Atheists, although it is convenient now to our friends to tell us—" Oh, no ! they were not Atheists !" I urge that all growth towards the overthrow of theological error, whether conscious or unconscious on the part of the individual, is Atheistic in its tendency and its consequences. I do not pretend that every man is capable of becoming an exponent of Atheistic thought—I do not pretend that he always knows the tendency of his own thoughts; but I believe there are many religious people who put lightning conductors on the steeples of their churches without knowing that it is a scientific Atheistical defiance of God in protecting the building by the agency of nature's laws. Now permit me to press this matter a little more fully upon my friend; and I ask you who are offended, or likely to be, with what you may think extravagant on my part, to remember that the only utility in debate can be that the men on either side express their views clearly and distinctly. If you have determined beforehand that I am wrong, if that is the decision you mean to abide by, then it is perfectly useless you coming here at all, if you cannot sit as a jury, and listen to what is to be put on either side—whether you belong to one church or another, this is not a fit place for you to come to at all. I ask those who taunt infidelity, those who taunt Atheism, those who ask me to prove *that* Atheism, to listen to me patiently. Take for example the investigation of the causes of poverty as an Atheistic work. I ask our friend how, upon any principle of the existence of God he accounts for poverty in the world at all? Either poverty is in spite of God, or because of God; but it cannot be in spite of God, for if you take the Bible you are told that that which He fore-knows is fore-ordained, that which is fore-ordained is predestined. But if God predestined poverty in the world did He fore-ordain it? Did He fore-know it? or has it happened outside of His knowledge? If so, where was His omniscience? Where was His omnipotence? Where His infinite goodness? Those who remove evil from the world must be those who do not think there is a Being who is doing all that is necessary in order to remove it. I urge therefore, when we direct ourselves to the lessening of crime, to the removal of disease, to the grappling with poverty, and to try and investigate its cause, and trying, however ineffectual it may be, to promote its cure, that we are as atheistic as man can possibly be, because our doctrine then is, we don't believe there is a ruler and guider of the world, who guides it as happily as it could be guided, because we fancy we see ill which we can remedy, when we understand the conditions upon which the ill rests, the removal of which will remove the ill with it. (Applause.) So far from shrinking from such a platform, it is the platform I have preferred to occupy all my life through, and ever since I learnt to think at all rightly. I have neither fear nor shame in the avowal of my Atheism. You burned 250 years ago a man for Atheism, and the only reason religion does not burn a man to-day, is because human progress has strove onwards and destroyed the power and scattered the faggots with which religion protected its weak defences. (Loud Applause.)

Rev. A. J. HARRISON.—It appears to me that Mr. Bradlaugh is trying to take the lead in this debate instead of taking his position and replying to me; and I contend that Mr. Bradlaugh, as a disputant, has no right to do any such thing. The proposition that I came here to discuss, I stated with the utmost clearness, is: "That Secularism, distinctively considered, is not a system of truth, and, therefore, cannot justify its existence to the reason." That was the proposition, and Mr. Bradlaugh informs me now that I have taken this proposition, and that I have discussed this question, because of his attacks on my faith, and the like. I want to know where Mr. Bradlaugh got his information from? I contend that Mr. Bradlaugh has no right to ask what my motives were, or to impute to me motives about which he can have no certainty. But, do you want to know why I have done this? I never thought the faith I hold needed defending in this way; it was enough for me to teach it, and then leave it to defend itself. (Cheers.) But the reason I have come to discuss this subject to-night is, first, because I have studied this matter of Secularism with a view to discover what there was in it of positive teaching, which I, as an independent man, might logically accept; what there was in it of other teaching that I could also accept; and I came here, not for the purpose of defeating Mr. Bradlaugh, but to attack Secularism, from the study of which I found that whatever it professes to have of positive teaching, it has, only in common with all the world—in common with all the world of humanity, that believed in science; and when Mr. Bradlaugh assumed that Theists could not believe in science, he only repeated Dr. Lardner's celebrated argument about the steam engine over again, who said that steam engines were impossible. But there are thousands of steam engines actually running on our railways, and Mr. Bradlaugh has told you that, logically, Theists must be opposed to progress, and that in order to progress he must be an Atheist. Well, now, I think the fact that hundreds and thousands of God-believing men through this and other countries believe in God at the same time that they believe in science is a sufficient answer to

Mr. Bradlaugh's statement. He says they cannot, but they do, and that is sufficient to show that they can. Now, certainly, I have no desire to consider this a matter of a fight in any other sense than as a conflict of opposite opinions, out of which a clearer light may be thrown upon those who hear. Mr. Bradlaugh has not proved that there is anything positive in Atheism, and I invite him to remember the meaning of Atheism as he himself has stated in the "Debate." Let him prove that Atheism has positive teaching, for all that he has proved yet belongs to science and not to Atheism. (Cheers.) Mr. Holyoake admits that it cannot have positive teaching; he (Mr. H.) says something to this effect; that it is merely a speculation concerning the existence of God, and being only a speculation in this subject it has no positive teaching. Well, now, Mr Bradlaugh, of course, may have his own opinion on this subject; but Mr. Holyoake may be right. But in the interests of common sense, and of the true use of the words, what does Atheism mean? It means a being without God. Well, I ask how a being without God has anything in it? How it has I cannot say. I showed Mr. Bradlaugh that, but he did not reply to that part of my former speech; that Atheism might be either of doubt, of ignorance, or of denial; that from ignorance, doubt, and denial, he could not build up positive teaching; and all the answer he could give me was by reading several extracts. (Cheers.) The real question we have to discuss to-night is, not that to which Mr. Bradlaugh is constantly referring — the question we have to discuss is not Christianity, but Secularism. My position may be stated in a few sentences. It appears to me perfectly absurd and illogical to discuss the question of whether the Bible comes from God, or whether Christianity comes from God, with a man who will not admit that there is any God to give the Bible, or any Christ to save the world. (Loud cheers.) We must first be agreed in admitting the Divine existence. When Mr. Bradlaugh admits that there is a God, when Mr. Bradlaugh admits the necessary logical preliminaries, then I will go on with the discussion of that other subject. (Applause.) Now, Mr. Bradlaugh states that he did not say that no possible conception of God was opposed to progress, but that none of the preached ideas of God were in harmony with progress, that all these were opposed to progress. When the Theist ventures to affirm that his God has an existence other than and separate from a so-called material universe, then the Atheist in reply says—"I deny the existence of such a being;" and, of course, Mr. Bradlaugh denies that there is a God at all. I assert that out of this denial there emerges no positive teaching; out of this denial nothing that can be relied upon. I stand here to-night and affirm that when Mr. Bradlaugh tells me I must be an Atheist in order to progress, it is about as logical as to say that in order to enjoy the light, a man must refuse to recognise the sun. (Applause.) I think whatever his view may be, it could not serve any good purpose to assume that all those who do not hold his atheistic conceptions were necessarily opposed to progress—logically considered at least. I take this position in the matter personally. I believe honestly and sincerely, with the whole force of my intellect and heart, in science as a marvellous revelation of God. I believe in man, I believe in the human mind and the human heart; and I believe in mental philosophy as a yet more marvellous revelation of God in human nature. I say that my Theism is perfectly consistent with both. All the different sciences become to me more precious, and not the less so, because I believe that they are direct manifestations of God. (Loud cheers.) If you take first of all chemistry, which appears to unfold to us the very elements of which all things exist, then I myself say, that chemistry as a science is more precious to me, and I honour it not the less because it comes from God. Then take mechanics, which gives the laws of solid matter, and the same remark equally applies. Dynamics, too, I value not the less because it shows the power, the wisdom, the intelligence of the God we worship. I say, then, that if you pass through the sciences onwards— through pneumatics, through optics, through electricity —you have the same thought so grandly suggested by chemistry, carried on through all : that they all declare the varied power and wisdom of God. And if you will pass further from nature in this form, to animated nature, if you take the different sciences that range through organized matter, the same thoughts arise. Botany ranging over the globe, describing all vegetation of all climes, breathes upward to heaven, from depths of leafy shade, from deepening vales, from open verdant plains, the fragrance of His name, who has crowned the hills with waving forests, gemmed the valleys with incense-breathing flowers, filled the fields with the gracious harvest, whose grain is the "gold of God;" zoology with its dependencies of anatomy and physiology, displaying every form of animal life, from the zoophyte up to man, acknowledge Him who has created the leviathan and the insect, and sees His glory in both ; while geography, describing the whole surface of the globe, testifies how excellent is the name of the Lord in all the earth. So also as to the history of the earth, geology going back to the creation, down to the foundation of the earth, writes on the rocks its testimony for God. And beyond the sphere of earth, astronomy—recording the movements of the heavens—I do not the less believe in, because the stars are to me

"For ever singing as they shine:
The hand that made us is Divine."

(Loud Applause.) What I contend for to-night is this : that when Secularism professes to say that disbelief in God, or, at all events, the witholding of belief, is necessary to the enjoyment of science, then I say that Secularism manifests either the most amazing ignorance, or the most astounding presumption. (Applause). But what right has any man to make this wholesale charge upon his brother ? We do not meet upon this or that creed, but upon the ground of common humanity, and I think he has no right to make any such charges against me, or against any man, when he is utterly incapable of proving them. I believe in science as much as any man, and I believe, moreover, that the man who refuses to obey the revelation of the laws that science gives him concerning nature, is an infidel to God, an infidel to nature, and is the enemy of man. (Cheers.) And it by no means follows that, because I believe in the lesser, I do not believe in the greater; that because I believe in science I do not believe in theology; or that, because I believe in theology, I must not believe in science or philosophy. I start from science and philosophy; I pass from the material universe to the study of man's nature, and then I come to the grand and comprehensive theology, and I find a personal Power in all, full of wisdom, and, through the cycle of the ages, governing this great universe. (Loud and prolonged cheering.)

Mr. BRADLAUGH.—It is somewhat curious that the only point which our friend has not troubled to debate this evening is the point of the principles of Secularism, as contained in the declaration of the National Secular Society. But while he chooses to read from the 17th page the work that we are to do, I challenged him to the 13th page, and in his speeches following, he has carefully refrained from even recognising the fact of their existence. And yet he asks me how dare I say that he is here against Secularism. Because Secularism attacks his Christianity. How dare I say it? Because the second of the four declarations is:—"That the theological teachings of the world have been, and are, most powerfully obstructive of human improvement and happiness." That is our declaration, and we hold that the more you teach theology, the more you impede and hinder human progress. Our friend says that is an insult; but then am I to strike out of my speech every assertion that seems an insult to my friend, because, if so, we had better not have debated at all. If the statement of the differences of opinion is an insult, what is the use of discussion at all? I think our friend needs more debate. When these insults come oftener, he may get well accustomed to them, and no longer feel insulted by them. (Hisses and interruption.) I am sure you need it a great deal more, for you never hear Secularists hiss your advocate, although he calls us "a compound of gross ignorance and presumption," which, I suppose, was a pleasant Christian-like way of putting it. (Ironical cheering.) He only said it would be "gross ignorance and presumption" if I did something, if I did something which I did do, namely, to state that the belief in Deity, as it is held, is inconsistent with human progress. I do allege that; and if that is "a compound of gross ignorance and presumption," I must lie open to that censure. But Secularists feel strong enough in their position not to mind a few adjectives, while you seem to think the adjectives of more consequence than the arguments. Our friend says that out of denial of God's existence there arises no positive assertion; an Atheist says :—"We have recourse to our knowledge of the conditions of existence, which knowledge we (like our friend) call science, and we learn that by the application of that knowledge we may avert results which you, as Theists, say are not avoidable, because they are in the hands and care of God." But he does not apply his belief to the cure of disease; he does not trust in God to cure it. He uses his lancet, and he uses his medicine, and he relies on the material means instead of the spiritual means, which had not done, nor were able to do it. You believe in man. I know of man. You do not believe in the phenomena of which you take cognizance; you know them; and yet you tell me to believe in what you tell me of something of which you tell me nothing, except in round and flowery phrases, which, when you come to test them, come to nothing. You have talked very prettily, but excuse me for saying, very absurdly, about "the stars" singing to you about God's existence. It is possible they may do that to you, but they don't to me— (hisses)—nor am I sure that singing of that kind will make your brain clearer, or understand better the position to be debated. I think that kind of preaching would be better left out for the rest of this debate, because I came here, not for the purpose of hearing you talk round phrases, which would do well enough in the pulpit—(hisses and disapprobation)—all I can say is, that if in this debate you are to dictate to me what is to be my fashion of replying, the end of the debate will be very different from the beginning, because then I shall not care even if I outrage your feelings, which at present I have striven to respect. You don't mind outraging mine, why should you have a monopoly of the outrage? Why, if my opinions are in the minority, why if you have God on your side, why if you have all these forces, why cannot you let a plain man say what he has to say in his own fashion? (Cheers.) At present no coarse phrases, nothing so coarse as that of "a compound of ignorance and presumption," have fallen from my lips. And, I ask you, how can you expect me to believe that my Secularism is worse than your religion, until you show me that your conduct is better than mine? (Loud cheers.) I must say that each such interruption is a lesson to me of the truth of the position which the National Secular Society takes, "that theological teaching is most powerfully obstructive of human improvement;" and I accept all this opposition as evidence in favour of this truth, and as a refutation of our friend's—(hisses and uproar)—there's another interruption breaking out again—(renewed disapprobation, and a voice—" Hold your tongue")—at any rate Secularists have been "improved" enough to keep quiet, but the religious people cannot keep quiet, because they feel indignant at the weakness of their own creed, when a blow is struck upon it. (Renewed hisses.) There's another piece of demonstration—(loud cries of "Question.")

Col. PERKINS.—The time is running away, so don't interrupt for the few minutes which remain.

Mr. BRADLAUGH (resuming.)—Our friend asks me how can our Atheism be positive, how can a man without God have any positive teaching? I will tell you. In politics he is positive enough, for while Theists teach God put the king on the throne, Atheists try to find out how the king came there, if it was best he should be there, and if not they try to displace him. In the same way, there is not one of the ills of society, which the Theist, as such, can grapple with, so long as he believes that society is regulated and controlled by God, for it would be another attempt at blasphemy to interfere in any way with it. But every man who endeavours to improve the conditions of this life is atheistic, in so far that he puts it that there is no Divine government which our friend spoke of in his last speech, that there is not that harmony, that Divine intelligence, that infinite goodness. The Secularist sees men who are wretched and miserable, and devotes his attention to remedy their position, and to prevent others from being as wretched as they are. That is positive work; it is no mere negation, or, if it is a negation, it is a negation of wrong and falsehood, which is a negation of that which hinders and obstructs human kind. And it is the absurdest of all begging the question to say there were hundreds and thousands of people believers in God. If the argument is to be put in that way, taking it as a matter of numbers, you will find there are 500,000,000 of people believers in Buddha. I have come here to night to hold that my Atheism must be as boldly spoken for as the most fashionable religion about you. I don't care if the assertion be the veriest insult that you can conceive, for if it is an insult that you cannot bear, then this is no place for you; it is time that you should be going to your chapels and churches, and listen to your teachers, until you are prepared to hear me tell you, as I tell you now—(interruption, and—"Tell us something about the question," "hold your tongue," and "put him out,")—I must say that this is the first time I have ever felt it necessary to show want of respect to a Newcastle audience; I have always in my life been treated here with true fairness, and I cannot conceive why, when you have so talented an advocate to defend your views, you really cannot leave me to waste my own time, and to bear my own punishment in my own case; for nothing can be more monstrously impertinent, or more cruel than your present conduct. And really, if I wanted to make one plea for the existence of the National Secular Society, it is that the bigotry of religion is so strong among you, that you cannot even hear a man express his own opinions, entirely different to yours, without giving vent to an outburst of passion and invective which you would regard as cruel indeed did it come from our side as against your own. (Loud cheers.) The time which the Chairman tells me I have, and which I trust you will permit me to use in my own fashion, is now so short that I can do nothing more in it than point out that, so far as this debate has gone, my friend has done two things: he has entirely avoided the principles of the Secular Society, and only dealt with their work; and second, when challenged that the application of that work is atheistic in its existence, has entirely failed to grapple with one of the propositions, and simply said that I wanted to lead the debate instead of following him, and urging that while I am to defend my Atheism—for he says it is my Atheism he challenges me to defend—he considers it an insult when I assert that progress and improvement are incompatible with the belief in an all-wise and an infinite Deity. That is a belief, I hold, which is simply impossible. Their minds cannot grapple with the conditions around them, because they must admit that, if an all-wise Being had planned everything, then all improvement was impossible on their part ; that those who strive for the improvement of society, that those who strive for the breaking of men's political fetters, must be men who either don't think that God has done anything, or who don't think that God is able to do anything, to make society fit to live in. In conclusion, I ask you—if you wish to convince Atheists, and win them to your side—to show them that fairness and that candour which they accord to yours. (Loud applause.)

The Rev. A. J. HARRISON.—I rise for the purpose of moving a vote of thanks to the Umpire, for his impartial conduct in presiding over this meeting. I am sorry that Mr. Bradlaugh had not a more patient hearing. I beg also to include in the motion, that our thanks be also given to the two Chairmen for their services this evening. (Cheers.)

Mr. BRADLAUGH.—I have extreme pleasure in rising to
second the vote of thanks to the Umpire. I saw him for
the first time to-night, and I am sure he has done his best
to make the discussion as fair and pleasant as could be. I
have great pleasure in seconding the vote of thanks to him,
and should still have greater pleasure where he the sole
President to-morrow night.

The vote was carried by acclamation.

Col. PERKINS briefly responded, and the meeting broke up.

SECOND NIGHT.

—)o(—

PROPOSITION :—" THAT SECULARISM, DISTINCTIVELY CON-
SIDERED, IS NOT A SYSTEM OF MORALITY, AND IS, THERE-
FORE, UNWORTHY OF TRUST AS A GUIDE."

Col. PERKINS.—Ladies and Gentlemen: The enthusiastic
reception you have given to the disputants shows to me
that the questions at issue are receiving deep and earnest
consideration on the part of all present. (Cheers.) I
hope and trust that you will accord, as last night, to both
of these gentlemen, who exhibited so much skill and talent
in the handling of perhaps as difficult a question as can
possibly be discussed,—I hope you will accord to them
the same attention, and the same respect as last night.
(Hear, and cheers.) In order that there may be no mis-
understanding whatever as to the conditions of the meeting,
and for the information of those who were not here and
heard those conditions read last night, I may state that
there were originally two questions for discussion, one of
which was before the meeting last night, and was as follows :—" That Secularism, distinctively considered, is not a
system of truth, and, therefore, cannot justify its existence
to the reason." Mr. Harrison supported this proposition,
and Mr. Bradlaugh was in opposition to it. This evening
the text for discussion is :—" That Secularism, distinctively
considered, is not a system of morality, and is, therefore,
unworthy of trust as a guide." Each disputant will be
allowed half an hour for his opening speech, and fifteen minutes for each subsequent speech, the discussion to be
continued for as nearly two hours as possible. [After ex-

plaining a matter of business to the meeting, Col. Perkins proceeded :—] There is only one other point to which I will refer. Last evening, on several occasions I noticed that there was an enthusiastic infant somewhere—(laughter)—which made itself so very audible on one or two occasions as to indicate that, at some future period of its existence, it will occupy at this end of the hall, the same prominent position which it occupied at the back last night. (Renewed applause.) As I have come to the conclusion that that child in arms, "distinctively considered,"—(roars of laughter)—cannot take a deep interest in Secularism, I must beg that the enthusiastic parents of that young infant—(laughter)—who took such a deep interest in these proceedings, should it give any further indications of either satisfaction or dissent, that its parents will, without calling in the aid of the police—(loud cheers)—forcibly eject the enthusiastic infant from the building. (Cheers.) With this slight digression, which you have received with so much good humour, I will now say that Mr. Harrison will be introduced by his chairman, and I trust that the meeting will disperse with the same good feeling as apparently it has opened. (Loud applause.)

Mr. W. Turnbull.—Mr. Umpire, Brother Chairman, Ladies, and Gentlemen : I have great pleasure this evening in once more feeling it to be my duty to call upon the Rev. Mr. Harrison to open the debate, and in doing so I have only one remark to make, and that is, it may seem to some of you that there is something like unfairness in Mr. Harrison having to open out the discussion on each evening. In reference to that I have only this to say, that this arrangement is not at the instance of either disputant, but that, with others, it was made by the joint committees who were entrusted with the entire of the preliminaries. With these few remarks I have great pleasure in introducing to the meeting, the Rev. A. J. Harrison, in whom I have very great confidence. (Cheers and laughter.)

Rev. A. J. Harrison.—Mr. Umpire, Messrs. Chairmen, Ladies, and Gentlemen : I suppose we all understand, with perject distinctness, what is the subject for debate this evening. Col. Perkins, " distinctively considered," is a very able Umpire, and there is no mistake concerning the clearness and accuracy with which he states his views on any subject whatsoever, even though that subject be an enthusiastic infant or an enthusiastic parent. It will be distinctly understood that I am not here to-night for the discussion of any other proposition than that which has been already named. (I don't know whether there will be any repetition of the attempt to-night to introduce the subject of Christianity, but I have to say in reference to that matter, what I said before, that I must of necessity keep to the proposition that I have already named, and which Mr. Bradlaugh himself accepted,—(hear, and cheers)—" That Secularism, distinctively considered, is not a system of morality, and, therefore, is unworthy of trust as a guide." For the sake of perfect clearness, and also that Mr. Bradlaugh may, at the earliest possible moment, be in possession of the information necessary for him to reply effectively to me, I will state in three sentences the method by which I propose to prove the proposition just stated. The first is, that Secularism professes to be a system of morality ; and secondly, that Secularism, distinctively considered, being confessedly Atheism, is not a system of morality ; because it has, in fact, no moral principles to offer ; thirdly, that because Secularism, distinctively considered, has no moral principles to offer, it is unworthy of trust as a guide. The first position I take this evening is, that Secularism professes to be a system of morality. In reference to this statement of mine, I would have you distinctly understand that I do not for a moment say that it *is* a system of morality ; I only assert that it *professes* to be a system of morality ; and in confirmation of that statement I will read to you from the fourth page of the Debate between Mr. Holyoake and Mr. Bradlaugh, and I trust that, at all events, I shall succeed this evening in stating with perfect clearness, what are termed Secular principles :—

1. Secularism maintains the sufficiency of Secular reason for guidance in human duties.

2. The adequacy of the Utilitarian rule, which makes the good of others the law of duty.

3. That the duty nearest at hand and most reliable in results, is the use of material means, tempered by human sympathy, for the attainment of social improvement.

4. The sinlessness of well-informed sincerity.

5. That the sign and condition of such sincerity are—Freethought, expository speech, the practice of personal conviction within the limits of neither outraging or harming others.

Now, allow me to say in reference to this question—which I say for the sake of perfect fairness—that this statement is given by Mr. Holyoake, and not by Mr. Bradlaugh, that there are certain things, in all probability, in this quotation with which Mr. Bradlaugh does not agree. Well, then, inasmuch as Mr. Holyoake, the founder of Secularism, is not to be taken to-night, whether as a responsible leader of Secularism or not, yet as the only public representative we have, I will read to you Mr. Bradlaugh's own words. On pages 28 and 29 of this same debate, Mr. Bradlaugh says:—

It is on the facts of the universe it (Atheism) gives its lessons. It is by the diffusion of real knowledge among the people, and the improvement of the people that Atheism does put out its scheme of morality. You cannot have a scheme of morality without Atheism. The Utilitarian scheme is an Atheistical scheme.

Now that is sufficient proof of the point for which the quotation was made, namely, that Secularism, as represented by Mr. Bradlangh, does claim to have a system of morality. Well, what is the difference between a scheme and a system? Perhaps Mr. Bradlaugh will tell me. I do not mean to say that it may not be possible to express a perfectly plain meaning by one not so plain. For instance, it may be possible to say that a chain is an elongated concatenation of consecutive links, but the word chain is very much simpler and plainer than that. Now, express the word system—or the meaning of the word system—by whatever word you will, that which claims to be a scheme of morality, must claim to be a system of morality, and that sufficiently proves my first position. (Applause.) My second position is,

" that Secularism, distinctively considered, being confessed-ly Atheism, is not a system of morality, because it has in fact no moral principles to offer." Now, in support of this proposition I ask your attention to several particulars, which I will endeavour to reduce to four sub-propositions, or state-ments. First of all, Secularism, being confessedly Atheism, is without any moral help that comes from the belief in God. Observe that I do not bring this forward as an argu-ment. I bring it forward as a statement— (interruption)— to clear the way for the argument that is yet to come. Secondly, that Secularism, being Atheism, is without any of the moral help that comes from the belief in immortality. The same remark applies here that I made in the first state-ment. The third point is that Secularism, being confessedly Atheism, is without the morality that comes from the study of human nature. Here is a very important point. I ask your attention to it, and I will put it into the fewest and simplest sentences. Once you pass away from Atheism, which is a negation, once you come to the study of human nature, Secularism, considered as Atheism, is at once given up, for when you come to the study of human nature you are no longer within the domains of Atheism, but within the domains of philosophy. In the fourth place I shall support this proposition by the statement that, if there be morality suggested by the processes of nature, as distin-guished from human nature, Atheism is equally without any help from that source. And, in confirmation of this view, I will read to you an extract from Mr. Bradlaugh's debate with Mr. Hutchings at Wigan. Page 48 of this debate says :—" My friend says, let us leave geology, astro-nomy, physiology, psychology, and ethnology, and then tell us how we are to know what is right. I can't. It is only by studying these, and by knowing the facts around you, that you *can* know what's right." Now, upon that statement I have two remarks to make. The first is that, assuming this to be true—or rather, the principle upon which the statement is based, then morality is not to begot out of Atheism—by Mr. Bradlaugh's own implied confession—it is not to be got out of Atheism, but out of geology, astronomy, physiology, psychology, ethnology, and the rest. And the second remark I have to make on this quotation is, that whatever may be the value of this rule, it appears to me to indicate, on Mr. Bradlaugh's part, an utter confession of morality with scientific knowledge. If Mr. Bradlaugh is prepared to take the position that morality and scientific knowledge are identical, and that they are in any sense convertible or interchangeable terms, then I am prepared to discuss that with him ; but I will put a fair meaning on what he advances, and will only ask him this . Are we to suppose that, if a man shall know the value and benefit of honesty, of truthfulness, of charity, that, in order to this he must know astronomy, physiology, psychology, ethnology; and so on ? (Laughter and cheers.) So then it appears to me that, even in these matters that I have indicated to you to-night, this position is absolutely unassailable, or at least cannot be assailed successfully, namely, that when Atheism gives you an appearance of morality at all, it is not obtained out of its Atheism, but it is obtained on the one side from the philosophy of human nature, and on the other from the science of the material world. (Cheers.) My third position is one that follows inevitably from the two positions I have already taken, namely, that because Secularism, distinctively considered, has no moral principles to offer, it is unworthy of trust as a guide. Now, I suppose that even Mr. Bradlaugh himself admits that, if the first two propositions are proved, the third will follow naturally enough. And now I will indicate to you the line of thought that I myself have pursued on this subject, coming to it neither as an Atheist, nor as a Theist, but as a man. I take it for granted that if you have a scheme of morality, you must obtain it somewhere or another. And I ask Mr. Bradlaugh this question, can he show me by what means a scheme of morality can be obtained from science, considered as distinctive from philosophy ; by which I mean the science of nature as distinguished from human nature ? Then let us come to the consideration of the nature of man, and see wherein we obtain our scheme of morality. I contend that we get a system of morality from the faculty recognised as

conscience, that intuitive and instinctive sense of the difference between right and wrong; something that teaches us,
for example, that it is desirable to be honest for its own
sake, and not simply because it is the best policy, for the
man who acts upon that principle is not an honest man, because he would be a rogue if roguery were the best policy.
(Applause.) For these reasons I say, that if you want to
determine your scheme of morality, you must inevitably
study the nature of man, and if the nature of man is con-
ditioned, is limited, and is improved by external nature,
then you are bound to study science, not independently of,
but in relation to, the nature of man. But when you have
done this you have been studying positive teaching all the
time, and not Atheism, which is simply a negation. If it be,
as Mr. Bradlaugh says, that you cannot have a scheme of
morality without Atheism—let me quote his exact words,
for I should be very sorry, even in the rapidity of an ex-
tempore speech, to misrepresent anything that Mr. Bradlaugh said; and if he can show me that I have misrepre-
sented anything, I shall be most happy to withdraw it—he
says:—"You cannot have a scheme of morality without
Atheism." Now, what follows from that? All of this
audience who are not Atheists are without a scheme of
morality. Well, now, it is quite possible to say that I do
make use of expressions very hard and harsh. Mr. Bradlaugh certainly does not say that about me, but at least, he
assumes it. But let me draw his attention to the fact that,
when he makes a statement of that sort—that without
Atheism you cannot have a scheme of morality—he is, in
fact, condemning nine-tenths, perhaps a very great deal more
than nine-tenths, of the very best men and women all
around us, as being without a system of morality; and certainly if I must be accused—though remember that my
conditional charge of ignorance and presumption was not
made against a person, but against a system—all that I can
say is, that if it be impossible to have morality without
Atheism, that is a far greater insult to the consciences and
conduct of this great audience assembled here to-night,
than any word that ever yet left my lips. (Applause.)

Moreover, clearly understand that I never said—I don't now say—that Mr. Bradlaugh or any other Atheist is without morality. That is not my position. I take the position of common humanity, for I stated frankly enough that a man may have a conscience, may seek to do his duty to his fellow men, and yet be an Atheist. But I say that it is all done as a man, and not as an Atheist. That is the position I have invariably taken. It is not my business to judge any man : I don't stand in the position to speak condemnation as to the sincerity or otherwise of a man's motives ; that I leave for the future tribunal in which Mr. Bradlaugh does not believe. But this much I do say. As far as I am concerned I take every man as I find him and understand him. If I find him to be an honest man I say so, whatever his creed or no-creed may be. And I do affirm this, most positively—not that Mr. Bradlaugh has no morality, for that would be a very gross, personal insult—but I do affirm that in his character and in his position as an Atheist, he is absolutely without morality. (Cheers.) That is to say, from the very nature of Atheism, you cannot extract any morality whatever ; that Atheism from its own nature, and from the very conditions of its existence, is without morality. Well now, you will ask me perhaps to repeat so much of my argument as will make this last point perfectly clear. Atheism, as I explained before, is either doubt, or ignorance, or denial. Well then, I said that you could not build up a system of truth from ignorance or denial, for it has no positive teaching, and it is not possible to extract a moral system from it. And if Atheism, as I have shown before, has no truth in it, I want to know how it is possible for any man to extract any moral scheme, or any scheme of morals from that which is, at the best, doubt or denial, or—let us take the medium between the two—ignorance ? (Hisses.) Now I have put it simply and solely upon this ground : If Atheism be something positive, then certainly the word Atheism is a misnomer, because Atheism indicates a negation only, and if Atheism be but a negation, then nothing positive can come out of it, because out of nothing nothing can come. (Applause.) And for that simple reason it is utterly preposterous to suppose that morality can come from Atheism. Well, this is the ground I take, and it is the position I am prepared to maintain in this night's debate. And whatever other questions be before us, I hope you will believe me when I say that my charge is against Atheism; and I do trust that you will understand that I am not attacking your character as a man—whatever your creed may be—but I am attacking that Atheism which I have described to-night, and also last night, and therefore attacking Secularism, seeing that Secularism is confessedly Atheism neither more nor less. I am glad to find I have a few minutes yet to spare, and I will occupy the time in putting before you this argument in another light. I contend that the Atheist, in his character as an Atheist, has no rights whatever. Now this seems a harsh statement, but remember whatever Mr. Bradlaugh's views may be as an Atheist, they cannot destroy his rights as a man. I take this firm and clear ground that the Atheist, as an Atheist, has no rights whatever, that the rights which he possesses are on the positive ground of his humanity, and not on the negative ground of his Atheism. (Applause.) That being so, I take this further position, that assuming Atheism for the moment not only to doubt or deny the existence of God and the immortality of the soul; but assuming further, that Atheism also denies what is termed the freedom of the human will—but which I prefer to term moral freedom—then a chain of argument may be very well constructed on this basis:—That where there is no freedom there can be no responsibility; that where there is no responsibility there can be no morality; that where there is no morality there can be no duties; and where there are no duties there can be no rights. (Loud applause.) Now I say, if I am wrong in this assumption, I shall no doubt be set right by Mr. Bradlaugh; but that is the position I am quite prepared to take, and to meet him upon. But I do meanwhile maintain that Atheism does deny human freedom, that it does deny the freedom of the will, that it does assume that circumstances and organizations leave men absolutely no choice; and that being assumed,

I ask Mr. Bradlaugh to follow the line of my argument in the way I have already indicated in that chain of thought presented to him. Let us recapitulate for a moment the propositions taken in my half hour this evening. I say then first of all, *not* that Secularism is a moral system, or has a system of morality, but merely that it *professes* to be a system. Secondly, that Secularism, distinctively considered, being confessedly Atheism, is not a system of morality, because, in fact, it has no moral principles to offer. And thirdly, because Secularism, distinctively considered, having no moral principles to offer, it is unworthy of trust as a guide. Well, I did not—in my speech itself, in the main substance of it, I mean—dwell so much on that point, "being unworthy of trust as a guide;" but I assume that moral systems set themselves up as guides. I take it for granted you do not want a scheme of morality at all if that scheme is not to guide you in the way you should live. And, if I have shown you that Secularism, distinctively considered, has no moral principles, I think I have sufficiently shown to you that Secularism, so considered, is unworthy of your trust as a guide. I have not gone into side issues on this part of the argument, and I hope you all understand the precise ground of debate to-night. I have only to add, that if Mr. Bradlaugh has anything to object to in this, that certainly is not my fault, and if he has anything to object to in my speech now, I hope he will, with all his energy, with all his ability, keep in substance to the propositions I have laid down. The proposition was sent to him for acceptance some weeks ago, and being accepted by him, he is not in a position now to discuss anything else than the proposition laid down to-night. (Cheers.) I maintain, moreover, that Mr. Bradlaugh to-night, is not at liberty to take the course he did last night, and that he is not at liberty to say he will not discuss whether Secularism be a system or not, for that is one of the very parts of the proposition we came here to discuss. (Cheers.) And, therefore, I claim to-night that Mr. Bradlaugh answer my assertion, that Secularism professes to be a system of morality, and will not pass away from the subject, bnt will discuss whether it be a system or not; and if Mr. Bradlaugh confesses it is not a system, then it must certainly follow that its name is hypocritical, for it professes to be what it is not. (Loud and prolonged cheering.)

Mr. J. WATSON.—Mr. Umpire, Brother Chairman, Ladies, and Gentlemen : When I look round this hall to-night, I am satisfied that there is a great amount of satisfaction and pleasure beaming from the countenances of all I see before me. I have no doubt that you have all, to a considerable extent, been exceedingly pleased with the manner in which Mr. Harrison has addressed you. I have been .pleased with you that you have listened to him so attentively. I have now to introduce to you the other disputant. Can I say too much when I ask you to accord to him the same patient and impartial hearing that you have accorded to Mr. Harrison. (Cheers.) And I do this not merely as his right, I do it simply because he is a man, and because he is here as a disputant in connection with the subject which has been chosen for discussion here this evening. Therefore, hearers as you are, you are bound to listen to the arguments which he may advance. I know there are a number of you who will feel very sore at many of the remarks he may make, but, as his Chairman, I beg of you to give him a patient hearing. (Applause.)

Mr. C. BRADLAUGH.—Mr. Umpire, Messrs. Chairmen, and Friends : Last night it was my friend's duty to prove that Secularism was not true, and to-night it is his duty to prove that it is immoral. He has taken one course only to support both propositions. He says, "Secularism is Atheism, Atheism is a negation, and that, as a negation, cannot be true—a negation cannot be moral." Well, then, he is good enough to mark out for me the line I ought to pursue in this debate ; and he says, "While I tell you that Secularism is a negation, I decline to allow you to say what it is a negation of." Now this is the very thing I intend to do : I intend to justify the negation by showing that it negates falsehood, and substitutes truth in the place of it. (Applause.)

Our friend omitted last night, while he dealt with Secular work, to refer in the slightest degree to Secular principles; and to-night, although he had these before him again, he carefully avoided dealing with that which lies at the root of our position, namely, " that the theological teachings of the world have been, and are, most powerfully obstructive of human improvement and human happiness." And our friend in effect says, " I won't permit you to say what theological teachings are obstructive of human improvement ; I won't permit you to say what theological teachings are obstructive of human happiness." That is, he likes to cut out a great portion of my defence ; he likes to put for me precisely what I shall not say, because he says the only thing I can say is to say negation, which is nothing ; and then he says, " out of nothing make something." I don't pretend to that cleverness, but I do pretend to stating my own views on this subject, utterly regardless of any sort of line my friend may have chosen to draw out for me. (Applause.) And besides, he told you that which of itself would have justified the course I intend to take, even though I had not intended to take it this evening. Without that justification, he says, Atheism is without the moral help of God, and without the moral help that comes from the belief in the immortality of the soul. He did not trouble to tell you how that moral help came ; he treated that as a matter that must be assumed for this debate. Now, it is just one of the things that I am not going to assume ; it is just one of the things I am going to attack ; it is just one of the things I am going to justify my Secularism upon. Now, our friend has raised one standard of morality which, permit me if you please, to dispose of entirely to clear the way for the ground I shall take He puts to you a conscience—an intuitive sense as to right and wrong, which he did not take the trouble to prove ; he assumed it as a matter which is incapable of doubt, and which is incapable of negation. Well, that is one of the things I deny, and I will trouble him when he addresses himself to it again, to tell me whether what he calls conscience is not simply the result of organization by education—meaning by education every surrounding of the human being—and whether conscience does not vary amongst different races of men, and in the same man in different stages of his life. (Cheers.) And I utterly deny intuitive ideas and intuitive knowledge at all; and I should like a few illustrations of them to enable me to judge what my friend means by them. I know of no ideas save those derived through the medium of the sensitive ability. I know of nothing prior to perception; I know nothing except a consciousness of present perception, or memory of past perception; and I allege that what you call conscience is a state of mind determined by the range of perceptibility, determined by the range within which it is exercised, determined by the effort of memory— perception determined, in fact, by the *tout ensemble* of that which you call the intellectual perceptibility of man; and I do utterly deny any intuitive knowledge at all. (Cheers.) When my friend talked of the moral help from God, I confess I was placed in this difficulty: if he has a notion of morality derived from a moral help in God, why do men steal at all? Are these men whom God don't help? Then they are wicked in consequence of His not helping them. That is the very doctrine of Christianity which I negate, and it is because I find that immoral doctrine that I am here to plead against it to-night. Our friend was good enough to wind up with what I suppose he thought, and no doubt many of you thought, a very eloquent denunciation of Atheism, by saying that Atheism had no freedom of will, or no " moral freedom," and therefore no responsibility— having no responsibility, no duties, and, having no duties, no rights. Why, my friend knows that Christianity at this present moment teaches that man has no such moral freedom, for in the 10th and 17th Articles of the Church of England—(hisses, interruption, and " Question ")—in the 10th and 17th Articles of the Church of England—(renewed hisses)—that in the 10th and 17th Articles of the Church of England—(great interruption, mingled with hooting)—that in the 10th and 17th Articles of the Church of England, which are part of the theological teachings to which Secularism objects, and which are obstructive of human happiness in this country—(hisses and " Question ")—that in those articles it is taught that it is utterly impossible for man to do good without God helping him to do it; that some men are predestined to do good and others predestined to do evil. (Disapprobation.) That is my friend's own doctrine. If so, a Christian Theist has no freedom; he has no responsibility, no duty; he has no rights. (Applause.) But I will carry this matter farther still, and I will tell you that Secularism is a negation; yes, it is a negation of the system of morality taught in this book, because when Secularism tries to teach men to be good husbands, the theological teachings of the world are found to be most powerfully obstructive to it, because in this book he is taught that a man may take a woman and keep her as his wife for a month, and then, if he is dissatisfied with her, turn her out to go where she will. (Hisses and hooting.) Secularism teaches him that the theological teachings of the world have been, and are, most powerfully obstructive of human happiness and human improvement. It wants to teach a man to be honest and truthful—honesty was one of the positions our friend took up—and how can he do it when he finds a liar and a thief like Jacob rewarded by God, while the man he cheats was hated and turned out? (Applause and hisses.) Our friend was right in saying that our system is a system of negation. We negate such doctrines as that, and endeavour to destroy them; we are endeavouring to destroy the Theism that teaches and supports them. Our friend asks you in his speech—"What has honesty to do with ethnology, with physiology, psychology, and geology, and the rest?" It has a great deal, and so much so that, when a man has disease of the brain, you don't convict him of theft, or of any crime he might commit, although his act is what you call stealing; but you know he is not the same man because of it, and because of your psychological knowledge you come to no judgment upon it; and while in the time of Jesus they would have said that he was possessed of a devil which made him steal, now you say he is an insane man—either organically insane, or insane by temporary disease—and you send him to a lunatic asylum to be cured, or to be guarded against his incapability. Our friend is right in saying that

Secularism is a negation, and he has pleaded in his speech that Atheism is deficient in morality, because it is without moral help from God. Why, what sort of moral help from God can you have when I find that a man who was a thief, a liar, a perjurer, an adulterer, and a murderer, like David, is held up by God as an example for others to follow and copy ? (Applause.) Why, sir, if these round phrases are only to be used, and I am to be told that Secularism is a system of negation, but I am not to tell you what it negates, why you had better bid me to debate with a gag in my mouth. Then our friend says Atheism is nothing but a system of negation. There he is wrong, for it not only negates, but it affirms. It affirms not one mighty universe, and a vacillating God outside, as you do. (Interruption.) Mind, it is not my introduction ; our friend introduced the moral help from God in his first speech—(applause)—and if I can show, as I shall show, that the God from whom he expects help is vacillating, is uncertain, does not Himself know what is to happen, changes and repents the line of conduct He has marked out, thinks to do evil and then retracts,—I ask what sort of moral help to straightforward conduct can you expect from such a source as that ? (Hisses and loud applause.) The difference of the proposition of the Atheist is, that he does not affirm a universe, and outside of that a God, but says—" By your knowledge of the conditions of existence, so you may shape and so will be shaped your conduct, and that thought and that conduct which tends to the greatest happiness of the greatest number, and to the least injury of any, that thought and that conduct are moral, whatever your religious profession may be." But that guide to morality is not got from any system of Theism : it is purely Atheistic—that is, it is formed outside God, without God. But our friend says—" I address myself to this question as neither an Atheist nor a Theist, but as a man." He pleaded also about the immortality of the soul, and the moral help of God, as the guiding props in his morality. Now, what is the position ? Secularism is a negation, because Secularism finds the theological teachings of the world powerfully obstructive of that scheme of morality ; for the theological teachings of the world say that the best men are the best believers, not the best doers: "He that believeth and is baptised shall be saved; but he that believeth not shall be damned." (Hisses.) But when I ask whether good works are wanted, I am told no; a man shall not be judged by his deeds, but that it is by faith, and by faith alone, that a man can be saved. But when my friend tells me that I will find morality outside of religion, I tell him that it is no defence of the theological teachings of the world, and it is to the theological teachings of this country that I object, because I find it clearly declared—

Rev. A. J. HARRISON (who rose to a point of order, amidst mingled cheers, hisses, and cries of "Sit down.")— I rise on an objection. We have an Umpire here to-night, and what is he here for but to rule on a point of order? My objection is that Mr. Bradlaugh is discussing Christianity, and not Secularism.

Mr. BRADLAUGH.—My answer is—(hisses)—if you have anything to say to order, I will sit down and wait. (Renewed hisses.)

Rev. A. J. HARRISON.— All I wanted to add was, that I did not wish to interrupt Mr. Bradlaugh, and if the Umpire overrules my objection, I will not urge it.

Mr. BRADLAUGH.—The objection taken is, that I have been discussing Christianity, and not Secularism. But to ascertain whether that be true, you must see the nature of my friend's proposition. His proposition is, that Secularism is a negation: it is a negation of something, or it is a negation of nothing. If it is a negation of nothing, there is nothing to discuss; but if it is a negation of something, surely I have a right to say what that something is, and I was showing that it was a negation of the theological teachings of the world, and I submit I was perfectly in order, otherwise there would be no debate at all. (Cheers and counter cheers.)

Col. PERKINS.—I think, gentlemen, that at this stage of the proceedings we should bear fully in mind that the discussion is, that Secularism is not a system of morality. Now, coupled with Secularism the question of Atheism has been placed. Now, I really think that the tendency of the discussion is to run into a comparison of the benefits between Atheism and Theism. (Applause.) I think that Mr. Harrison is right—(cheers)—in what he says in the position he takes with regard to his argument against the general proposition of Atheism; and I think that Mr. Bradlaugh should confine himself strictly to the discussion of Theism. There are many forms of Theism, and I don't think that Mr. Bradlaugh should select one section of Theists, those being Christians. (Hear and applause.) I don't think he should select one section from the great mass of Theists who exist in the world, and I hope, therefore, for the future he will confine himself as much as possible to general Theism rather than to one section of Theism, which is Christianity; because a Jew and a Unitarian are both Theists, as the case may be, but their divinity is of a different character to that of the Christian. I think Mr. Bradlaugh should confine himself to questions generally of Theism, which will be better than selecting any one portion from amongst the number of Theists who are in the world. (Applause.)

Mr. BRADLAUGH.—I accept the ruling, as I am bound to do, of the Umpire, but permit me to point out to you that, according to the Umpire's own ruling, I am doing what was perfectly right, and I will show you why. I am told that I must confine myself to Theism; but there is Buddhist Theism, Brahamanistic Theism, the Theism of the Persians, the Theism of the Unitarians, the Theism of the German and some of the Rationalistic schools; but I intend directing your attention to some of those special forms of Theism in this debate; as our friend would say, I have nothing to do with it, and, therefore, I took that phase of Theism which was nearest at hand—that phase of Theism which an Act of Parliament says I must take—Christian Theism—by which I am liable at any time to be indicted if I deny it, and, taking the Act of Parliament as my guide, and the Chairman's ruling, I may adhere to Theism; but I take Christian as being the most proper phase of Theism to deal with. Then what position are we in? I will endeavour, as carefully as possible, to resume our argument at the place I left it. I was dealing with our friend's notion of moral help derived from God, and the faith involved in it, and that I find in Christian Theism faith is put higher than conduct, faith being the test of morality instead of conduct, and so much was that so that in the final exposition of Christian Theism I am told that they are to be accursed who presume to say that every man shall be saved by the law. (Interruption.) Really, Mr. Umpire, this is pertinent to the question; it is as pertinent as Charles Watt or George Jacob Holyoake. If you may read to me George Jacob Holyoake to explain Secularism, surely I may explain to you your Act of Parliament, your form of Theism as contained in articles of the Church. I did not object to your quoting J. P. Adams, and don't you object to my quoting the Bench of Bishops: " They also are to be accursed that shall presume to say that every man shall be saved by the law or the sect which he professeth, so that he be diligent to frame his life according to that law and the light of nature. For Holy Scripture doth set out unto us only the name of Jesus Christ, whereby men must be saved." Now, I say that that entirely upsets the whole position taken by my friend. He says, "I come to you as a man, neither Atheist nor Theist." That is what he cannot do. He did not separate himself from Theism. In the course of his very opening speech he tells you that Secularism is a negation, and he is in a terrible way for fear, I suppose, that I will tell you what it contradicts, to declare not to be true, to deny, to destroy, and he does not want me to tell you what I want to destroy, what I want to declare is untrue. He wants to have all the talk on his own side, and then to claim a glorious victory. Why, if my friend had known anything about Secularism he would never have framed this patent question-trap in which he thought to catch me. He said, " Perhaps Mr. Bradlaugh will object to the words of the question." Mr. Bradlaugh has done nothing of the kind; he has not troubled himself to object. I saw that they were meant very cleverly to catch me and shut me up; but I do think that, at least, our friend should have been prepared—especially when he talked of my being the President of the National Secular Society—to discuss the very principles on which that very National Secular Society is based, namely, that the theological teachings of the world have been, and are, most powerfully obstructive of human improvement and happiness. Now, there is one of the theological teachings of the world which is purely Atheistic. What is one of the theological teachings of the world which, I allege, entirely interferes with man's happiness? I answer, the moral doctrine of special providence. Take this instance : You have a fire in a coal-pit, 300 people are killed, and three are saved, and you actually thank God for His providence in saving the three, as though He thought it was a matter in which you desire to express your praise and approval. Why, if there is anything in it at all, you ought equally, according to your own doctrine, to allege blame against God for destroying the 300, who would be just as much destroyed by His own act in the one case as the three were saved by His own act in the other. Now, what is the position the Atheist takes? Why, he says God don't explode mines at all; an Atheist says explosions are the only result of certain conditions, and if you learn what those conditions are, then you are able to prevent them, and God will not be able to cause them. (Applause.) Atheism is not only a system of negation, as it not only negates the wicked and blasphemous doctrine that God has blown up a mine; but it also affirms that, by ignorance of the conditions of the elements he is dealing with, man may avert such ill effects for the future. Then again, as to the question of morality, while the Theist always teaches that the regulation of the forces of the world is in the hands of God, and when we (Atheists) go into the quarters of the poor, the miserable, and the wretched, and finding their poverty, finding their crimes of society, we are met by my friend, who says that these poor have moral freedom, that they may choose not to starve, that they have moral help from God to prevent them from stealing, and that they have moral help from their belief in the immortality of the soul, which will prevent them from picking pockets. But the Atheist says, a man born in this condition, his organization has driven to his bed, and that crime is as much the outgrowth of the condition in which he was born as the mushroom is the offspring of the midnight soil. Well then, you see that our doctrine is not a doctrine of negation alone; it is a doctrine of negation and affirmation, and I don't wonder that one did not approve of my telling you what we negate. Secularism affirms the doctrine of social equality, and that it is possible to get men organized, and trained, and cultivated in fraternal relations; and that equality between man and man is possible. But we find that the theological teachings of the world are obstructive of that union and that equality, because it is one of the doctrines of Theism, as taught by the Bible, that men may buy and sell slaves, may breed them and keep them as slaves for ever; and allow me just to inform you, in passing, if the fact mentioned by William Wilberforce in his speech made in introducing a bill for the abolition of West Indian slavery —you will find that William Wilberforce reminded the House of Commons that infidel France had set an example to Christian England by setting their slaves free first. But, says our friend—and he seemed to think it clever as well, but it only shows how men's notions will differ as to what is clever—he says the only reason an Atheist may be honest is on account of its being the best policy. But I will tell you that it is not so. An Atheist who studies the conditions of existence never will think so, because he finds that mischief follows mischief; and further, that doing a good makes good, and that it is good, and at the same time the best policy to do good. (Applause.) What did my friend mean?—I confess I did not understand what he did mean, or whether he simply said it to give any sort of force or weight to his position—what did our friend mean by telling me that, as an Atheist, I was without the moral help of God. unless he would permit me to criticise the character of the God whose moral help he said I was without? Why, if

I find God, who has promised to protect the Jews, who has brought them out of the land of Egypt with the intention of protecting them, when I find Moses made laws for them, God being utterly unaware that they were relapsed into idolatry; when I find God suddenly becoming angered and determined suddenly to destroy them all—" Let me alone that my wrath may wax hot, that I may destroy this people" —when I find Moses remonstrating with God, and find God repenting him of the evil he thought to do—I ask how can I derive any moral help from such a God as that? (Loud applause.) I hope and trust, when our friend comes to deal with this question, he will no longer shirk those principles, but deal with them, and show that he has not overlooked them wilfully. He tells me and you what he would permit to be done in this debate; but I tell you that I come here the advocate of the weak and the poor—(ironical cheering) —I come here the advocate of the poor; I come here to free Atheism, to free Infidelity, to free Secularism from that weight of public and conventional feeling which you have exhibited to-night, which starves poorer men than me, and drives them into disingenuousness, because that they have only misery if they dare be honest. (Loud applause.)

Rev. A. J. HARRISON.—I must pray you not to express your approval or disapproval during the quarter of an hour I have to speak. My friend Mr. Bradlaugh thought I was in a terrible fluster; now I ask you to look at Mr. Bradlaugh, and then say which of us is in the most terrible fluster. (Laughter.) Now there is one particular point I wish to refer to at once. When I rose I did not want to interrupt Mr. Bradlaugh, but Mr. Bradlaugh invited me to get up.

Mr. BRADLAUGH.—That is not true; it is utterly untrue; it is utterly untrue.

Rev. A. J. HARRISON.—You see Mr. Bradlaugh—(uproar)—if Mr. Bradlaugh—(more disapprobation)—if Mr. Bradlaugh will remain quiet, he will see no need for the remark. I wanted to speak to a point of order. Very well. Mr. Bradlaugh must not lose his temper. Mr. Bradlaugh must be patient, and he must hear me out and not interrupt me. And now he must see that my object was very much different to what he supposed. Mr. Bradlaugh invited me to get up, and I did so. Well now, I think when this debate is printed, as it will be, you will be able to judge yourselves how far Mr. Bradlaugh has touched my positions. (Applause.) He tells me of this "patent question trap." Well, there is no trap in it. When men set a trap they don't give notice three or four weeks before-hand. I sent my propositions to Mr, Bradlaugh, and he knew perfectly well what I was determined to discuss. And I would ask :—Does Mr. Bradlaugh know anything in this wide world about logic or not ? (Mr. Bradlaugh :—Yes.) He answers yes; and I accept the answer. (A voice :—" Do you know ?") Very well, he accepted the proposition that Secularism is not a system of morality, and is, therefore, unworthy of trust as a guide. What does Mr. Bradlaugh undertake to prove ? His position is to prove that it *is* a system of morality, and that it *is* worthy of trust as a guide. (Applause.) How does Mr. Bradlaugh attempt to prove this ? He tries to make out that something else is as bad as Secularism, and therefore—by this amazing logic—Secularism is good. (Laughter and applause.) I am amazed that any man of sense can argue in that way. All I can say is, that if Mr. Bradlaugh follows the same line, I must absolutely decline to continue the discussion, that's all. (Interruption.) However, I will reply to so much of Mr. Bradlaugh's speech as does not attack what he calls Christianity. (Applause.) He began by saying that I alleged that Atheism is immoral. I alleged no such thing. I confined myself to literal exactness in saying that it is not a system of morality. Has Mr. Bradlaugh so much as tried to prove that it is ? ("No.") Mr. Bradlaugh, moreover, tells me that Atheism negates falsehood and substitutes truth ; but does not his logical sense tell him that that which substitutes truth ceases to be a negation, and therefore, the very moment that Mr. Bradlaugh substitutes truth he ceases to act as an Atheist, but acts simply on the ground of the positive teaching that I have described. If Mr. Bradlaugh is not willing to answer me in this position, and if, instead of doing so, he submits certain questions of his own, he has no right to assume for a moment that I am afraid. I am not given to boasting, but I must defend myself from an imputation of that sort. I leave to Mr. Bradlaugh the monopoly of " bullying," and I decline to follow him in that. If Mr. Bradlaugh will speak without so much passion in the matter, he will do well. (Applause.) I say then, that I have not shirked the principles of Atheism, because I have proved that Atheism has not got any principles to offer. Moreover, I find that Mr. Bradlaugh is guilty of the very thing he charges me with. (Laughter and applause.) Now, I pray you to observe how ingeniously Mr. Bradlaugh makes the remark—I will withdraw the word " ingeniously," and will simply draw your attention to Mr. Bradlaugh's blunder. He said that I had stated that I derived moral help from God, and the like. Well, if I had said it, it would have been a fine point to have taken up, but I will tell you what I said—I do not introduce this matter here as an argument at all, but simply as a statement to clear the way for the argument. (Applause.) Or, as Mr. Bradlaugh's memory appears to be so short, I will repeat that part of my argument to which that was the preface. My position was that you were taking morality from the positive fact, namely, humanity, and, therefore, in taking it from humanity you came into the region of mental and moral philosophy, and that is not Atheism. My position was that in so doing, he was acting simply as a student of mental philosophy, and not as an Atheist. Moreover, Mr. Bradlaugh has never shown yet, that every possible form of Theism is opposed to progress, and if he has not proved that, he has proved nothing to the point. I pray you further to notice Mr. Bradlaugh's logic. in answer to what I quoted as to the sciences. Mr. Bradlaugh said " they had a great deal to do with honesty," and, as an instance, quoted disease of the brain. But allow me to tell you, that if you take this ground that because a man has disease of the brain that therefore you will hold him guilt-less of any crime while he acts under that disease, you imply the very same moral law I contend for in that very statement. (Applause.) Then what is it but some princi-ple that tells you that because a man has disease of the brain he is, therefore, not responsible? How Mr. Brad-laugh shirks this question of responsibility! The moral principle says that a man being under the influence of dis-ease of the brain is not responsible, and, therefore, is not to be blamed. Where then do you find this element of re-sponsibility? You find it, as I have already indicated, from the study of man's mental and moral nature; you do not find it in the positive sciences at all. I ask Mr. Brad-laugh again whether Secularism has some positive teaching or not. He says my proposition is a "trap;" but the ques-tion is—is my proposition correct or not? Does he confess that he cannot answer it? If he cannot, what is he doing here to-night? (Applause.) When I was invited by the Newcastle Secular Society to discuss with Mr. Bradlaugh, I said at the time I would discuss Secularism, but would not discuss the question of Christianity; and when Mr. Brad-laugh charges me with setting a "trap" for him, he ought to have been a little better acquainted with the facts; his committee ought to have posted him up in the matter. There is no "trap." I simply put into a few words the views I hold concerning Secularism, and Mr. Bradlaugh was logically bound to prove that Secularism, distinctively con-sidered, was a system of morality, and, therefore, worthy to be trusted as a guide. He was bound to prove the affirma-tive while I took the negative, or else decline to discuss at all. I ask this audience to observe that Mr. Bradlaugh has given us nothing about Secularism to-night. He has never told us what Secularism is. He has given no justification of it, but he allows judgment to go by default. Mr. Brad-laugh so far, if he does not do better before the close, has confessed himself absolutely defeated. (Loud applause.) I ask the attention of the audience to the fact that the Se-cular leaders cannot defend their Secularism; they cannot find anything in it to defend, but they have to run away from it to attack Theism, and especially Christianity. (Applause.) All I have to say upon the matter is, that whether Mr. Bradlaugh holds himself logically bound to the terms of the debate or not, I do. I have far too much respect for my own reputation, for my own consistency as a reasoner, to depart from the strict terms of the debate. (Applause.) Moreover, I ask Mr. Bradlaugh to say, whether he considers it altogether courageous in him—when I am bound not to defend Christianity by the very terms of the debate—whether he considers it courageous in himself to attack it? (Applause.) Now, I hold myself to these positions I have taken—the three main positions—and not one of these positions has Mr. Bradlaugh even condescended to notice. I hope that he will at least endeavour to make something of them when he gets up to speak to them again. I don't need to say more, because if Mr. Bradlaugh goes on in the course he has been pursuing, of course I am exempted from any further discussion. (Loud applause.)

Mr. BRADLAUGH.—May I again call the attention of my friend to the principles of the National Secular Society, whose leading proposition declares that "the theological teachings of the world"—(strong manifestations of dissent)—I compliment my friends on the " bullying"—(hisses and "Question")—may I again call his attention to the proposition involved in the principles of the National Secular Society, which he asserts he came here to discuss, which are that "the theological teachings of the world"—(derisive laughter and hisses)—I cannot help asking every one here to bear with me while I read one sentence from my friend's last speech. He says : " Mr. Bradlaugh has not shown that every possible form of Theism is opposed to morality." He must first of all do that to show that no possible form of Theism is opposed to morality. I must at any rate begin with some form, and I have taken the Christian form. (More interruption.) I don't wonder that you repudiate it. (Hisses and "Stick to the question.") Our friend's whole contention—(renewed hisses)—well, if you won't listen, I'll talk to the reporters. Our friend's whole contention was, that Secularism was a negation, and evidently he expected me to show what I negated, for he put it that I was bound to negate every possible form of Theism. That was his own declaration in the speech to which we have just listened. (Interruption.) I cannot make humanity for Christians; I can only appeal to decency; if they don't possess it, I can only regret that you teach me here a lesson to-night which I am sorry to learn. (Applause.) If I am defeated, it will be far better to allow my defeat to appear upon the pages of the report than to show that when, by the admission of the other side, the victory was won, they could not allow the defeated man even to say something in his own defence. (Applause.) I have been asked the question whether, if I were in a meeting where I had authority, and any Infidel interrupted a Christian, would I put him out? I tell you that I myself would, and have turned men out of the room; I have done so repeatedly in my life, and I don't understand why, if you feel so sure that you are the best, the truest, the most logical, that you cannot in addition be the most patient. (Cheers and hisses.) The Secularist, finding faith put higher than conduct, objects to such teaching, as being calculated to impede human progress, and he teaches, on the contrary, that human faith is not dependent upon any such freedom of volition as our friend talks about, but is the result of organization and education, and is no more a matter of morality than the colour of his skin, the character of his nationality, or the height of his body. It teaches that it is by conduct and the effect of conduct that morality is to be judged, and hence it is that it is obliged to attack the theological teachings of the world, because the Theistic teaching is, as I have already pointed out, directly at variance with it. Atheism says there is only one existence of which you know the conditions. If you only learn those conditions step by step, and day by day, you will find that each additional day's knowledge will give you additional help to be more useful to yourself, and to be more useful to your fellows; that is, more moral and more free. The Theist, on the contrary, says that it is not so; he says there are certain laws of morality unalterable, fixed, intuitively revealed,

But our friend has not troubled to deal with that at all, while he has challenged me with neglecting that point in the debate ; but when the debate comes to be read, it will be found that he has carefully avoided the points at issue from the beginning to the end. He has only run out a form of words about negation, very noble in their way perhaps, but the meaning of which we are utterly unable to comprehend. (Hisses and ironical cheering.) Why, he says that when Atheism ceases to be a negation, it is no longer Atheism ; but he has taken upon himself to determine what Atheism shall be. Let us try it by his own ideas. He says that because Atheism ceases to be a negation, it is no longer Atheism. Why, how have I described it (Atheism)? It negates God ; it says : "There is the universe, study it, apply your knowledge to render your life in it more complete, more true, and more honest, and you can do all that without God, and we can show you how to do it." That is what Atheism says, and if that be not affirmative Atheism, then I do not know the meaning of my word. (Loud cheers.) Well then, our friend says he did not introduce the moral help of God and the moral help of the immortality in the argument, but to clear the way for the argument. Why did he introduce it at all? If to clear the way, then I attack it to clear it out of the way. (Applause.) If it be only so much rubbish, it should not have been put there ; if it was intended as a weapon, I was right to deprive it of any power. I cannot say that my appreciation of the intellect of my friend, or the fairness of his supporters, has been increased when I find the popular feeling against unpopular views erecting such a one-sided tribunal in your minds, for you not only determined what views I should take, but what I ought to say, to determine precisely the fashion in which I shall say it. You have no more patience than the Christians of 250 years ago had when they burned Bruno at Rome. (Hisses and interruption.) Why, what pleasure, what satisfaction can you derive in a mere series of unmanly yells? If these are demonstrations of your love, I should wish to be saved from it. Our friend said that I tried to prove that Secularism was as bad as Christianity, or that Christianity was as bad as Secularism.

I did nothing of the kind ; I tried to prove that it was worse. (Laughter and applause.) That it endorses lying, murder, theft, and adultery, all of which Secularism rejected. (Loud applause and hisses.) It does not arise as to whether I was right or wrong, but it does arise as to the line of argument I debate, and I am justified in saying—(interruption) —when our friend takes the trouble to be jubilant over the victory he thinks he has achieved, he might at least have waited for an impartial audience to decide. The general who cries victory before the battle is half over, is one who neither knows the strength of his ammunition nor the ability of his foe. (Renewed hisses.) Our friend says—I suppose he meant it—that he communicated with me about this matter some time ago. He may have done so, but I had never the slightest communication in my life from him. (Applause.) I have only communicated with the committee. (Hisses.) What does this mean ? I tell you I have not done anything of the kind, and you will not allow me to give my version of it. Surely if he may introduce a statement of the kind, I may give my view in reply ; and it is a most monstrously unfair thing to elect how much I shall say, and how I shall say it. My friend challenges me to say that, at least, one possible form of Theism is inconsistent with morality. He says that : "Before you can justify Atheism from this point of view, you must show that every possible conception of Theism is inconsistent with morality." Then I take one form of Theism, and I show that that form is entirely inconsistent ; and I put it to you, as I put it in my "Plea for Atheism"—"Cognising to take the phenomena of the universe seeks to apply its knowledge with a view to man's elevation, and to man's benefit, and to man's advancement, while the various forms of the world grope in the dark ; for they allege that outside the world there is a power which controls it, a power which made a hard and fast line of morality, which they say is to be found in the conscience, but a hard and fast line we don't find at all." I challenge my friend to define his own conscience ; I challenge him to show what he himself means by it. I showed you before my notion of morality, and there has been no one attempt made to deal with it; nothing but mere boast, nothing but mere braggadocio is supplied in place of arguments. I cannot help saying that, at least when I am asked whether Atheism is moral or immoral at any rate, I am reminded of the words of Bacon when he says that : "Atheism may lead a man to morality, though religion may not ;" and I am further reminded of the words of Samuel Taylor Coleridge, that : "There was not one man in a thousand who had strength of mind, or goodness of heart enough, to be an Atheist." I don't pretend that the words of these great men are any further or any greater evidence than mine or, any other man's might be ; but I put them to you to show that, at any rate, I do not stand alone in this ; and Atheism itself teaches, at any rate, that with so many religions in the world, with so many churches in the world, with so many chapels in the world, all cannot be right ; one must be wrong, or all may be wrong. It teaches human kind not to hiss a man because he is a Mahommedan, not to hiss a man because he is a Christian, not to hiss a man because he is an Atheist, but to take and examine his conduct as a man. And it tells you further that, while creeds quarrel, and religious people exhibit the malice of their creeds, human nature can work for its own deliverance, and in its own development. (Loud cheers.)

REV. A. J. HARRISON.—(Hisses and applause.)—I think our Secular friends are determined to prove that they also know how to hiss. Let us at all events try to conclude this meeting with as much good humour as we began it, and I hope that I shall be able to shake hands across the table with my opponent, and all go home in peace ; and now I pray you to observe what I have got to say in my last quarter of an hour, because it is of consequence that every word I say should be well pondered. My friend says I challenged him to prove that every possible form of Theism was opposed to progress, and so on; but that was not brought in as a part of my main argument, but as a reply to him. Moreover, Mr. Bradlaugh has referred to Bacon and Coleridge as being men who have uttered those fine sayings concerning

Atheism. I know of Bacon's saying, but I did not know the quotation from Coleridge, or what relation it has to the context; but this I know, that both Bacon and Coleridge had strength of intellect and goodness of heart enough not to be Atheists. (Applause.) Mr. Bradlaugh contends that I had cried "victory" before the battle was over. I did no such thing, and Mr. Bradlaugh ought to know that. ("Question.") Is it not my business to reply to what Mr. Bradlaugh said? I say I stated no such thing; I said that if Mr. Bradlaugh refused to discuss the proposition I gave him, that Mr. Bradlaugh by that refusal would confess himself defeated—(applause)—and I say it now. Moreover, Mr. Bradlaugh says he received no communication from me. Well, at all events, if he did not, I am not responsible for that, but I will give you a word of explanation. As Mr. Bradlaugh intends it, he may be perfectly right; but, nevertheless, the fact is just as I stated. The committee having accepted, as far as they were concerned, the propositions, returned them to me, and I sent them to Mr. Bradlaugh, addressed to 29, Turner Street, Commercial Road, London, which, I suppose, is his correct address. Of course it is quite possible that Mr. Bradlaugh would not be aware that these propositions had come from me. The point is, whether he had received them in time to peruse them? (Applause and laughter.) Mr. Bradlaugh says there is an affirmative Atheism. Then he might as well have said that yes means no, and no means yes. (Laughter.) What do you mean by an affirmative negative, and a negative affirmative? I confess I don't know. I cannot comprehend his meaning when he talks about affirmative Atheism. In closing this discussion, allow me to express my very sincere regret that Mr. Bradlaugh has not been patiently heard. I am sorry for that, and yet there is as much logic in a hiss as in a clap; and when you allow your audience to express their approval, you must also allow them to express their disapproval. But I regret it upon this ground, that Mr. Bradlaugh has evidently been labouring under a very severe cold, and it would only have been kind on the other side to have allowed him to have gone on in quietness, so long as he attempted to confine himself to the question ; but when Mr. Bradlaugh, in such a way as he has done in his last speech, made such a charge against a Newcastle audience on account of their interruption of his speech, all I can say is, that he might easily have avoided it by discussing the propositions. (Applause.) Mr. Bradlaugh says that I have called Atheism and Secularism—for Secularism is Atheism—immoral. I simply said that it was without morality, and it was for Mr. Bradlaugh to say whether it was moral. Has he done it? ("No, no," and "yes," and interruption.) I will venture to affirm now that Mr. Bradlaugh—and he cannot say that there is any want of courage in my so framing it, he having the last reply both nights—I now say that, while I hesitated to say that Secularism was immoral, I venture to say that Mr. Bradlaugh himself has proved that it is immoral by his own argument. (Cheers.) Mr. Bradlaugh does, in effect, deny the possibility of sin—I will not insist upon that expression—but when he denies the freedom of volition, he denies the very possibility of morality altogether ; and if you only tell a man that everything he does is the result of his organization, and that he has no choice, then, as a matter of course, what he does is equally right or equally wrong, there is no morality at all ; and I say that is a positively immoral doctrine. (Cheers.) But remember that was not my argument, but Mr. Bradlaugh's own. And now I ask you, upon his own showing, what becomes of this boasted freethought? Let us apply this a little more. I will be merciful. (Laughter.) I ask you to consider what all this talk means, about freedom from creeds and the like? Well, I know this much, that Mr. Holyoake, when he is not writing as an Atheist, but as a philosopher, tells us that the creedless philosopher is quite at sea ; and if Mr. Bradlaugh is to be compared by Mr. Holyoake's standard, then our president philosopher is quite at sea. (Laughter and applause.) Well, then, if these different leaders of Secularism contradict each other, and are opposed to each other, that itself proves that the so-called system is unworthy of trust as a guide ; for so long as there are no definite principles, no creed by which to test the so-called system, you must appeal only to the views expressed by such men as Mr. Bradlaugh and Mr. Holyoake. Then again, in this secular organization you find such men as Mr. Holyoake, who—from the stand-point point which Mr. Bradlaugh takes—ought not to be a Secularist. But though they don't agree in things positive, they have a wonderful agreement in things negative. They don't agree in positive teaching, but they both agree in their being Atheists. I ask you now to consider how, in all this freethought talk, there is one particle of common sense, for either every man is a freethinker or he is not. If every man be a freethinker, then it is a matter of very gross impertinence for Secularists to claim that for themselves which belongs, at least, to all. (Cheers.) And if every man be not a freethinker, then he must, of course, be bound, and his bondage must be the result either of organization or of choice. If it be the result of organization, what becomes of their freethought? (Laughter and applause.) What sort of freethought is that which is necessarily produced by organization? But if his bondage be the result of his choice, then, at least, he must have been free, or he could not have chosen to be bound. But again, if he is bound, his bondage must simply be a bondage of error. If he is to blame for his error, then he must be responsible for his belief, which Secularists altogether deny. But if you deny his responsibility for belief, then, again, what becomes of your freethought? What business then has Mr. Bradlaugh to attack all these Theisms if we cannot help what we do? And if we cannot help what we do, then, I suppose, the only justification Mr. Bradlaugh has for his being here to-night is, that he could not help it. (Cheers and laughter.) And I have further to say, that I believe as much as Mr. Bradlaugh, or any other man in the room, in freethought; and I invite every Secularist to break off from him for ever the shackles that bind him in the superstition of his Secularism. (Applause.) I invite him to ascend the mountain of truth, to get away from the dull pestilent clouds around him in the dark vale in which he has chosen to dwell for a time. I ask him to get up to the mountain-top; I ask him to take the widest view he can to exercise his thought; I pray him to take in as much as he can of all the mysteries in the universe ; I tell him then that, in doing this, he is just a freethinker, as I am; for he that studies the truth is made free by the truth. It is not by passionate invective against creeds and against theologies—most of which were manufactured in Mr. Brad- laugh's own intellectual manufactory—it is not by passionate invective against this or that, that the truth is to be ad- vanced amongst our fellows here. I have laid down my propositions as plainly as I can, as free from all rhetoric, as free from all attempts of what Mr. Bradlaugh calls " pretty phrases," as my nature would allow me. My propositions were so clear that it was utterly impossible for any man to mistake them, and Mr. Bradlaugh has not dared to answer them. (Applause.) And I say now that Mr. Bradlaugh has, in effect, confessed that he could not answer them. (Applause.) And why ? I will tell you the reason—(hisses and applause)—why Mr. Bradlaugh has not dared to attempt to deny them ; it is because he cannot. (Applause, hisses, and " No, no.") I say that if he could he would have ven- tured to answer them before my last speech to-night, when I had no opportunity of reply. If he could have answered them, he would have had courage enough and manliness enough to have attempted to have answered them before ; and I pray you freethinkers here use, but don't make too free with the truth ; don't take liberties with the truth ; study the truth ; master it, know it, make it your own, love it as far as possible, be it, and then you are freethinkers in- deed : then you are freethinkers as I am, and just as those whom I represent here ; and my last words to you are : Judge for yourselves, take the so-called principles of Secu- larism and examine them, study Mr. Bradlaugh, study Mr. Holyoake ; and when you come to examine the so-called principles of Secularism, you will find the justification of my not having noticed what are called "principles of Secula- rism," in the fact that there are no principles in Secularism to be noticed. (Loud and prolonged applause.)

Mr. C. BRADLAUGH.—Our friend says that the argument that every possible form of Theism was not opposed to

morality, was not a part of his main argument; but if a part
of his argument at all, surely it was legitimate for me to address myself to it. Then he says :—Mr. Bradlaugh tells
me of negative Atheism, but when he tells me that he
simply tells me that yes means "no." Now really I cannot
imagine that a man with any practice of thought at all,
should have so thoroughly misunderstood and misrepresent-
ed what I said. I urged that Atheism denied the existence
of a God controlling the universe, but affirmed that man
should study the conditions of the universe, with a view to
applying his knowledge of these conditions to human improvement and human happiness, and I pointed out that
that was affirmation of a road to morality without God,
and of a morality without Theism. (Applause.) Our friend,
although he has in his very last words told you that you
would find that he had not touched the principles of the
Secular Society, because there were none, cannot forget that
in my very first speech I read the four principles from the
15th page of the Almanack, while he read the statement of
work from the 17th page ; and in every speech since I have
challenged him to deal with them, but he has been per-
sistently and utterly silent in relation to them. (Applause.)
I don't care—(laughter and cheers)—I don't care to do
more in this debate, at this stage, than on that point to leave
the printed report to speak for itself ; but I am bound to say
that I never met with a more utter evasion of the point we
have come to discuss. It is not at this stage a question as
to whether I am right or I am wrong in the principles I
advocate, but it was a question whether I urged any at all,
and whether Mr. Harrison has come here to discuss them.
And I declare that he was bound by his own view of it
to discuss the principles of this Secular Society, that had
been enunciated by himself, but he has utterly refrained
even from repeating, much more from examining them,
or dealing with any one of them, and the reason is—(interruption)—in mercy I ask you, in humanity I beg of you, or
if you have neither mercy nor humanity, then I impeach
you in the name of your religion, and show you how utterly
—(the remainder of the sentence was drowned by the cla-

mour of the audience.) Mr. Harrison urges that I, in effect, deny the possibility of sin. I don't deny it in effect; I deny it in plain and distinct terms. If God exists, sin is impossible; if sin exists, God is impossible. And I will take the definition of sin from the very man who, he says, was a good and pious Christian—Samuel Taylor Coleridge— I will take his definition, and seek to support my argument. Coleridge says: " An act to be a sin against God must be originated in the will of the actor, entirely apart from, and external to, all circumstances other than that will." And I put it to you, I don't deny it in effect; I deny it in terms as distinct and clear as possible. Well then, he is good enough to tell you that myself and Mr. Holyoake are at variance on everything positive. Is that true? If it were true, it would only be true as against two men, but not as against Secular principles. But have we been at variance in posi- tive work? Were we at variance on reform? Were we at variance in getting liberty for the Italians? Have we been at variance in getting the freedom of the Press? If that is not positive work, I don't know what is. (Uproar and " Question.") I did not introduce Mr. Holyoake into this de- bate, but he having been introduced, I have a right to show that, while we have our distinct and clear thoughts, we have our common work for human redemption and for the public good. (Applause.) And I put it to you here to-night, concluding this debate—I put it to you that, should you think me worthy of conversion, if you belive in the immor- tality of my soul, and consider it worth the saving, and are, at any rate, confident in the strength of your position, then you might at least have shown as much patience, as much kindness, as much courtesy, as you would have shown to be the fruits of that system which you tell me is so much su- perior to mine. (Applause.) Our friend speaks of freethought, and I put it if we had only dealt with the principles, he would have seen the barriers which we contend are in the way of freethought, the barrier first of the Act of Parliament which I alluded to in my very first speech, and which makes such thoughts as I hold penal. The barrier next is popular prejudice, which you have exhibited during this debate, and which makes social excommunication a blight upon any man with courage to attack you and your views; and these are the things which cramp and fetter thought. These are the things which make it petty; these are the the things which make it puerile; these are the things which make it childish. (Interruption and hisses). Why, bear with me a minute or two longer. Our friend tells you that he has not said that Secularism is immoral; he only says it is not morality. Is there any distinction? I confess I am not clever enough to discover it, because I have defined morality to be that which is the greatest good for the greatest number, with least injury to any. He has not quarrelled with my definition, he has not pretended it was wrong; and I say, therefore, that I stand here in the position of taking ground, which, according to my position, remains intact and unimpeachable; because, what is the first declaration of the National Secular Society? "That the promotion of human improvement and happiness is the highest duty." I have defined the promotion of human happiness to be the morality I have spoken of. Our friend has never challenged the definition given, nor has he quarrelled with the principle, but he has allowed judgment to go by default. (Hisses and applause.) I have only a few more minutes, and in those few minutes it would be the height of folly to introduce any more matter into this debate; and I ask you to judge of the position as it stands. In my commencement, I told you that the Secular Society takes the position of attacking the theological teachings. Our friend told you in his speech that Secularism is a negation, and I stated what it negates—the theological teachings of the world—and how it hopes to arrive at morality independent of them. Our friend, however, has never grappled with any one of these positions; he has only said one or two things which don't apply, and that he only introduced the argument to clear the way. Our friend has been good enough to speak of "bullying" in this debate, but I ask him quietly and seriously whether there has been any attempt to "cow" the utterances of the Christian advocate—to prevent him having full and fair play? I ask him if it be true that we were in the depths of the mire of ignorance, and whether we have not at least learned that humility which all men ought to have when they stand on the mighty shores of the Unknown? We don't pretend that Bradlaugh is right; we don't pretend that Holyoake is right; but what we do pretend is, that every man in the world has the right, when he finds a false system, which he thinks, rightly or wrongly, weighing down the world, hindering its progress, impeding its civilization, that then he has not only the right to denounce it, but it is his duty to denounce and attack it. If we are in error, if we are wrong, if it be true, as our friend puts it, that in immortality we are to be condemned for our presumption here, at least that doctrine should teach you to be more charitable, more kindly, and more merciful now, for if an eternity of torment awaits the Atheist for his denial of God, how petty must be the spleen that seeks to supplement God's vengeance by causing additional agony to a sensitive mind here. I plead not as a leader, but as an advocate. I do plead as a representative of man; I do plead as one who has won the right to plead, and I plead against the system which has wealth, which has fashion, which has power on its side; and I plead in the name of the advancing progress which has put infidels on your own bench of Bishops, which has split your Church asunder, and which is allowing science to go where religion hitherto stopped the way, and which, although it might fail to obtain a tolerant audience for Atheistical opinions, in the life of the speaker and of the Secularists present, may yet obtain—("no, no")—such a hearing in your grandchildren's days and mine; for the time will come when the people will be sufficiently honest, sufficiently free, and just enough not to hiss an expression of opinion different from their own, but, enlightened by the progress of the age, will afford to the honest expression of conscientious opinion that treatment which it demands in the present age in vain. (Mr. Bradlaugh resumed his seat amid loud applause.)

Mr. BRADLAUGH (again rising said :—)I have very great pleasure in moving a vote of thanks this evening—as Mr. Harrison did last evening—to the worthy Umpire who has

presided; and I will include the two gentlemen who have
officiated as Chairmen, and the Committees who have charge
of these proceedings. Whether the result of the debate
will be to win converts or not, I rejoice to know that it will
result in aiding some institutions which needed aid. And
I will add that I am especially obliged to the Umpire, whom
I met for the first time on this platform; and who, though
he may have listened to things which must have caused him
pain, has been just and impartial throughout. (Loud
applause.)

Rev. A. J. HARRISON.—I have very great pleasure in
seconding the vote which Mr. Bradlaugh has so admirably
moved. I am glad to be able to say that, in the very little
experience I have had in committees, I have never known
any committee work so harmoniously, as the committee for
arranging this meeting. I hope you will consider well what
has been said, and whether this discussion will influence
public opinion, or—as Mr. Bradlaugh expresses it—win
converts, of this one thing we are satisfied that Col. Perkins
has done his duty in the chair as Umpire, on both evenings
of debate; and I only hope that we shall go away in the
same good-humoured way in which we commenced. (Applause.)

The motion was then put by Mr. Bradlaugh, and carried
by acclamation.

Col. PERKINS.—Gentlemen: On behalf of the Chairmen
of the debating parties, and of the joint Committee, and on
my own behalf, I beg to thank you for giving such satisfac-
tory acknowledgments to us for the manner in which we
have discharged the public duty which we accepted volun-
tarily. A discussion of this sort is very difficult to conduct;
and I think that, considering the very delicate ground which
the enthusiasm and haste of argument, and eloquence, might
induce the contending parties to take up, that, upon the
whole, they have very fairly kept within the respective barriers or frontiers which divided the two countries of each

from the representatives. (Laughter and cheers.) I cannot, however, allow this meeting to close without frankly and honestly telling the audience which I see before me that I, individually, standing on that place which Mr. Bradlaugh has eloquently defined as the "mighty shores of the Unknown"—I must tell you that standing and contemplating creation, the universe, and infinity, and their unknown mysteries, which are so incomprehensible to my limited intellect, that I must take them rather as evidence of the existence of a Supreme Power than as evidence against it. (Loud cheers.) I would also say that I can not receive the action of an unhealthy condition of a man's organization as any proof that a healthy being is not responsible for his actions. (Laughter and applause.) With these two remarks, which I wish you to understand are simply personal opinions, I shall now disperse the meeting; and I think we may congratulate ourselves upon having received at the hands of the disputants a vast amount of intellectual raw material, which, I hope, we shall take home, and in the manufactories of our brain, work them up into a good commercial article— (cheers)—which will prove useful to ourselves and beneficial to mankind at large. (Loud applause.)

The meeting then broke up.

W. S. CROW, PRINTER, SIDE, NEWCASTLE-ON-TYNE.

www.ingramcontent.com/pod-product-compliance
Lightning Source LLC
Chambersburg PA
CBHW031454270326
41930CB00007B/1004